Toward a New Theology of Ordination

Toward a New Theology

of Ordination:

Edited by
Marianne H. Micks and Charles P. Price

Foreword by
John M. Krumm

Essays on the Ordination

of Women

by
Reginald H. Fuller
Frederick H. Borsch
Lloyd G. Patterson
Arthur A. Vogel
Urban T. Holmes
James E. Griffiss
Ruth Tiffany Barnhouse
Frans Jozef van Beeck, S.J.
Henry H. Rightor

VIRGINIA THEOLOGICAL SEMINARY
ALEXANDRIA, VIRGINIA

GREENO, HADDEN & COMPANY, LTD.
SOMERVILLE, MASSACHUSETTS

Permission to reprint "Patriarchy and the Ordination of Women" originally appearing in *The Nashotah Review* (Vol. 15, Fall, 1975 No. 3) is gratefully acknowledged. Material in that essay from Carl G. Jung, "Psychotherapy Today" in THE COLLECTED WORKS, ed. by Gerhard Adler, Michael Fordham, William McGuire, and Herbert Read (trans. by R. F. C. Hull) [Bollingen Series XX, vol. 16, copyright 1954 and © 1966] is reprinted by permission of the publisher, Princeton University Press.

Distributed by Greeno, Hadden & Company, Ltd.
Library of Congress Catalog Card Number: 76–634
International Standard Book Number: 0–913550–09–4

CONTENTS

FOREWORD

As the Episcopal Church prepares to decide at the 1976 General Convention about the ordination of women to priesthood and episcopacy, it is important that we see clearly the reasons based on scripture, theology, history and tradition to make an affirmative decision. The case seems to me, ever since I served as a member of a committee of the House of Bishops which dealt with this issue in 1971 - 1972, to be a strong and persuasive one. At the same time, I have become convinced that the arguments against it — insofar as they derive from scripture, theology and church history — rest on very dubious interpretations of those three major sources of authority in the Christian community. I hope these essays will be widely read. They have been written by careful and competent people whose experiences and scholarship entitle them to a hearing. They avoid over-simplification, which raises temperatures but casts very little light. Read these essays with a readiness to have the Spirit of Wisdom speak through them to your mind and heart and, whatever your conclusion, help us to carry on this debate, not with slogans and emotional rallying cries, but with reason and from deeply Christian conviction.

John M. Krumm
Bishop of Southern Ohio

INTRODUCTION

Fresh thinking about the meaning of Christian faith is imperative in every generation. The "faith once for all delivered to the saints" keeps ever alive and well provided we continually invite it to address the specific time and place in which we live and work, the specific problems about which we argue and pray. Whether or not you admire James Russell Lowell as a poet, he was right about "the cross that turns not back". Precisely because "that scaffold sways the future", we "must upward still and onward / Who would keep abreast of truth."

The essays collected in this volume are examples of such fresh thinking in the last quarter of the twentieth century, in a society facing an army of question marks about the future. All of the authors address just one contemporary question — why the Episcopal Church should or should not ordain women to the priesthood and episcopacy. Yet in their thoughtful answers to that question, they once again demonstrate how creative theology is born in the midst of controversy, and why any single theological issue opens up a wide range of Christian doctrines. God's truth is all of a piece.

It should not surprise us that controversy can sharpen thought. Many of the greatest Christian theologians turned their minds and their pens to very concrete problems plaguing the church in their day. St. Paul developed his ideas of law and grace because some Christians in Galatia were quarreling over the rite of circumcision. St. Augustine forever enriched the church with deeper insight into the meaning of baptism because of a violent disagreement with a fellow churchman named

Pelagius. We would know far less about Martin Luther's world-changing rediscovery of justification by grace through faith if he had not engaged in heated pamphlet warfare. With such precedents, we might well expect our present debate about the ordination of women to produce some enduring insights into the meaning of the Gospel of Jesus Christ. These essays stand in that mainstream of our tradition. Theology is not done in a vacuum.

The editors are excited about the wide range of theological issues which the contributors have discussed. Although the meaning of ordination is the central focus, the essays here presented invite you to think also about such matters as the Triune nature of the One God, the authority of Scripture, the significance of human sexuality, the fundamental purpose of ministry, the Lordship of Christ over his church. Thus they make a positive contribution to the entire theological process, as well as to the immediate question of who can or cannot serve the Lord in the ordained ministry of this branch of his church.

This collection is published, therefore, for three reasons. We believe it is an authentic model of Christians *doing* theology afresh for our generation. We believe it offers creative and constructive insights for a theology of ministry in general, a topic of vital importance to the renewal of the church. And, to complete the trinity, we believe that it will introduce its readers to some strong theological arguments in favor of ordaining, for roles of leadership in the church of Christ, some persons who happen to be female.

Marianne H. Micks
Charles P. Price

1 Pro and Con: The Ordination of Women in the New Testament

Reginald H. Fuller

Anyone who seeks to justify the ordination of women from the record of the New Testament has a difficult job. Jesus appointed only men to be his apostles, and Paul, it seems, was downright negative about women, going so far as to forbid them even to speak in church. If you regard the New Testament as a blueprint for all time, the case is settled and not worth arguing about. Let us here take a closer look at the New Testament evidence — both pro and contra — by four general categories: 1. Jesus; 2. The Earliest Church; 3. St. Paul; 4. Emergent Catholicism.

1. *Jesus*

CONTRA   The recorded calls of disciples were all of men (Simon and Andrew, James and John, Levi, and the unnamed would-be disciples).[1] Most modern scholars, a few Germans excepted, would agree that out of the wider body of the disciples Jesus in his earthly life chose Twelve for a particular role — to be signs of the New Israel that would come into being with the advent of God's kingdom.[2] The Twelve were men.[3] If Jesus intended his church to have women ministers, it is argued, he would have included women among the Twelve. After all, Jesus did not scruple to break the customs of society in his day by, for example, healing on the sabbath or consorting with outcasts. Surely, had it been his intention he would have appointed women. Instead, they performed the subordinate service of looking after the bodily needs of Jesus and his disciples — a sort of women's auxiliary.

ANSWER   Of course Jesus appointed only men. But was Jesus legislating for his church for all time? Even when the gospels were written, the early Christians continued to believe that the end of time was coming soon. And although they arranged the teachings of Jesus (especially Matthew in his five discourses) to make it look like legislation for the church, even Matthew still thought the end was coming fairly soon. Scholars are divided in their views of what Jesus thought about the end. Some of the best scholars say that Jesus expected a fairly short interval to transpire between his own death and the End,[4] while others think that he expected his death to be followed almost at once by the coming of the End,[5] which in a sense it was, on Easter Day. These are the only two views tenable in the light of modern scholarship, and on either view, Jesus was not concerned to legislate for his church for all time. When the early church came to work out its arrangements for the ministry it did so *without reference to what Jesus had done in his earthly life.* They proceeded under the guidance of the Spirit. That Jesus appointed only males among the Twelve says nothing about the ministry of the church today, for it said nothing about the ministry of the church in the period immediately after Easter.

PRO   Jesus was remarkably free in his dealings with women. Think of how he accepted the devotion of the woman who was a sinner (later, but mistakenly, identified with Mary Magdalene),[6] how he accepted the ministrations of women, — including Mary Magdalene — on his journey to Jerusalem, his encounters with the Samaritan woman and the woman taken in adultery. To have treated women fully and without reservation as *persons* was a remarkable thing in the ancient world, and particularly in Palestinian Judaism. There is nothing in Jesus reminiscent of the rabbinic prayer, "Blessed be the Lord who hath not made me a woman." It would be wrong to ascribe this to humanitarian broadmindedness. Where Jesus departed from established custom, as he did in consorting with the outcast, he did so because God's kingdom was breaking through in his own word and work, and that kingdom shattered the barriers erected under the law between men, and between men and women.

2. *The Earliest Church*

CONTRA   The Twelve forsook Jesus and fled at his arrest. But the resurrected One appeared to Peter and the Twelve and constituted them the foundation of the new Israel, as the earthly One had promised. The Twelve were all males, including Matthias, who replaced Judas. As the church began to expand, a larger number of "apostles" to whom the resurrected One appeared, headed up the mission. The earliest account of the Easter appearances (1 Cor 15:3ff) does not mention women because Paul is carefully listing accredited witnesses to the resurrection appearances, and under Jewish law women were disqualified from bearing legal testimony. There were no women among the apostles. True, there were almost certainly women among the 500 to whom the Lord appeared at one time (1 Cor 15:6), but that does not make them apostles. To be an apostle, one must not only have seen the resurrected One (as the 500 did) , one must also have been specifically called to be an apostle. As far as the leadership of the earliest church goes, it was all male. As in Jesus' earthly lifetime, women occupied a subordinate position of ministering to the needs of the community. And as the community grew, the same principle was adhered to. The Seven, who were leaders of the Greek-speaking community, were males. Later on when the apostles had left Jerusalem, James and the elders took over the leadership; but it is out of the question that there were women among them.

ANSWER   The situation of course is precisely what you would expect in a Jewish, Palestinian environment. At the same time there was a remarkable exception. The church believed from the earliest time that the tomb of Jesus was discovered empty by Mary Magdalene and some other women (the other names vary).[7] Of course the male disciples must have checked up on the women's story later. They were probably in Galilee at the time and so could not have been on the spot to check at once, as in the later accounts in Luke and John. That looks like a bit of male chauvinism! The women are not to be denied the importance of their testimony — and this in view of the fact that under Jewish law women were disqualified from giving testimony. It was a remarkable community which based its Easter faith — this essential part of its faith — on the witness of women.

3. *Paul*

Here we come to some very positive stuff and also the most negative in the New Testament, as far as women are concerned.

Let us take the negative first, for it is this that has figured so largely in the discussions about the ordination of women.

CONTRA   Paul taught the subordination of women to men: "... the head of every man is Christ, the head of a woman is her husband [NEB: woman's head is man], and the head of Christ is God" (1 Cor 11:3).

It is this statement which above all others incurred the oft-repeated charge (even before the term became popular) that Paul was a male chauvinist. On the other hand, efforts have been made to limit or explain away the implications of this text. Thus the RSV translates "her husband" rather than "man." Attractive though it is, it will not do. For in the context Paul is not talking about marriage but about public worship, not about the relations of husband and wife, but about men and women. Again, it has been suggested that "head" here means not superior authority, but source of being — the reference allegedly being to the story of Adam's rib. Again this will not do. The series, God-Christ-man-woman, indicates a descending order of authority. To interpret "head" as source gets us into serious theological difficulties: it would mean that Christ emanates from God in the same way as Eve from Adam, and that man emanates from Christ in the same way as the source of his being. Only "head" gives a consistent sense throughout.[8]

Another explanation has been offered to the effect that Paul is here talking about the situation of man and woman after the fall, when God punished Eve by placing her under Adam's authority: "Your desire shall be for your husband, and he shall rule over you" (Gn 3:16). We could then argue that in the Christian dispensation, when the effects of the fall are remedied, this subordination should no longer obtain. Quite apart from the question whether we can subscribe to the doctrine that the effects of the fall are entirely done away in Christ,[9] it is apparent from the context that Paul has man's *created* nature in view, not his fallen nature. Thus a few verses further on Paul says:

> For man ought not to cover his head, since he is the image and glory of God; but woman is the glory of man. (For man was not made from woman, but woman from man. Neither was man created for woman, but woman for man). — 1 Cor 11:7-9

Paul is giving a practical ruling: women prophesying (more about this later) are to be veiled. He bases his argument on

Gn 1:26 - 27, the creation of man in God's image, and Gn 2:7, 21 - 22 (the rib story). The same teaching about the subordination of woman to man is developed much further in the later New Testament, and we will look at it later. This is the strongest biblical argument against the ordination of women, for it is an exegetical and theological argument, not just a ruling (though it is adduced to support an *ad hoc* ruling, that women should be veiled when prophesying).

Later in the same letter Paul returns to the subject and issues a further regulation: "The women should keep silence in the churches. For they are not permitted to speak, but should be subordinate, as even the law says" (1 Cor 14:34). This presumably refers to Gn 3:16, where God says to the woman after the fall: "Your desire shall be for your husband, and he shall rule over you."

ANSWER.   At first sight, these passages, especially the one in chapter 11, pose a very serious problem. We may disregard the regulations Paul lays down about women being veiled and men not, for these have never been taken as an absolute rule. Bishops wear mitres in church, the canons of 1604 allow clergy with "an infirmity of the head" to wear skull caps in church, and until recently some Anglican priests wore birettas in church. At one time all women (not only those prophesying, as Paul directed) were covered in church, but within living memory this custom has practically gone by the board in all denominations. What is more serious is that Paul gives a *theological* reason for the subordination of woman to man. She is subordinate to him because God created man in his own image, and woman only from man. (Paul almost suggests here that woman was not made directly in God's image, but only reflects it from the man!). Unfortunately Paul used scripture here in a way no exegete today would dare to do. He combined two quite different creation stories, Gn 1:26 from P and Gn 2:7, 21 - 22 from JE.[10] As a result, he almost contradicted Gn 1:27, which insists that God made both male and female in his own image. From the P story alone you could not deduce that subordination of woman to man, but only that both actually bear God's image. Why did Paul believe in subordination? Not because he first read it in scripture, but because he first took for granted the mores of the society in which he lived, and then he looked around for a scripture text to justify it. Advocates of the ordination of women should not feel too badly when their opponents accuse them of capitulating to the spirit of the age (women's lib and all that). After all, Paul did very much the same thing!

As for the second passage, the contradiction with 1 Cor 11 is puzzling. In chapter 11 Paul allows women to pray or prophesy in church (but under a restriction: they must be veiled), whereas in chapter 14 he says roundly, no woman should speak in church at all. The answer to this puzzle is to be sought in the manu· script tradition. In some manuscripts verse 34 - 36 appear after verse 40. This is a sign that the passage was probably not written by Paul, but interpolated later. And it is the same rule as is found in 1 Tm 2:11 - 12. So it probably comes from the same hand that wrote 1 Timothy. We will give our answer to the problem of 1 Cor 14:33 - 35 when we come to deal with "emergent Catholicism."

PRO   It is remarkable that Paul envisages women praying and prophesying in church (1 Cor 11). He is not speaking about private groups, but about the public assembly of the church. It was prophets who presided at the liturgy in Paul's time, who offered the prayers including the eucharistic prayer (1 Cor 14: 16 — the Greek word for "thanksgiving" is *eucharistia*). It is therefore quite possible that at Corinth women did do just this! Yet Paul was not quite happy about it, for he placed a restriction on women prophets: they were to be veiled. Why? He offered theological reasons, which, as we have seen, are not convincing to scholars today. But there is something else at stake. Paul was very much worried about what is "proper" (1 Cor 11:13). People might be shocked at the goings-on in Corinthian worship so Paul tried to dampen it down a bit. Let the women be veiled! If what is "proper" is an important consideration in Christian worship, then what is proper (especially to the outside world today), may be the precise opposite of what it was in Paul's time: it may be an actual hindrance to the gospel that women are not allowed to lead public worship, while such leadership is accepted in other walks of life. At one time in Corinth the church far outstripped the world in the place accorded to women. Now some might accuse it of dragging its feet.

There is also the famous text in Gal 3:28: "There is neither Jew nor Greek, there is neither slave nor free, there is neither male nor female; for you all are one in Christ Jesus." Many attempts have been made to rule this verse out of court in the debate on the ordination of women. We are told that it refers to baptism, not to ordination. It is true that the immediate context is baptism, as the previous verse shows: "For as many of you as were baptized into Christ have put on Christ" (Gal 3:27). Paul fought a great battle for the first of his principles: the equality of Jew and Gentile in the church. At Antioch he resisted the attempt of the Judaizers to have "separate but equal" eucharists for Jew and Gentile (Gal 2:11 - 14). He would not have accepted the argument that it was all right because the Antioch church permitted Gentiles to be baptized! Paul fought that issue on the long view and he won. For no one today would doubt that Jewish and Gentile Christians may sit down together at the Lord's Supper. Paul did not make an issue of slavery in his lifetime, though in the case of Onesimus he did hope that his master Philemon would release him. He was content to transform the personal relationship between Christian master and Christian slave and let it go at that. Even so, he did not restrict the point to baptism. (See Philemon, and 1 Cor 7:21 - 24). But in the 19th century it seemed to many Christians that Gal 3:28 demanded precisely that they work for the emancipation of slaves. To say that so long as slaves were admitted to baptism that was enough would no longer do.

Today we are in the same position with regard to the relation of men and women in the life of the church. Society has developed in such a way with women's equality of educational opportunity that to refuse ordination *now* (whatever was the case in Paul's time) is no longer compatible with Gal 3:28. This is a fundamental statement that far outweighs Paul's negative statements about the place of women in the church.

But that is not the whole story. Paul had a number of women colleagues. He refers to Prisca, with her husband, as his "fellow workers", the same word he uses to describe Apollos (1 Cor 3:9), Timothy, and lesser known colleagues like Epaphroditus (Phil 2:25) and Clement (Phil 4:3). He speaks of Phoebe as a "minister",[11] the word he uses elsewhere of his own apostolic ministry, and of the ministry of his colleagues.[12] There are also Euodia and Syntyche (Phil 4:2 - 3) and Junia (?), Tryphaene, Tryphosa and Persis (Rom 16:7, 12). It would be an anachronism to ask whether they were ordained. Modern scholarship, both Catholic[13] and Protestant,[14] is agreed that ordination as such did not come into the church until after the time of

Paul.[15] We can certainly conclude with recent French Roman Catholic scholars that "Paul is much more positive — much less of a misogynist — than is generally thought."[16] That Paul was able to break with the conventions and customs of his age and culture to such an extent can only be due to his strong sense of the newness of what had come in Christ, to what modern scholars would call, in their jargon, "realized eschatology".

4. *Emergent Catholicism*

A few years ago a young American scholar published a paper with the intriguing title, "What Became of Paul's Eschatological Women?" We might rephrase it and ask why was it that the church soon abandoned the freedom with which Paul approached the question of the ministry of women. We are now dealing with a number of documents which, though purporting to be by the apostles and belonging to the apostolic age, nevertheless are now widely acknowledged to belong to a later generation. Such writings are: Colossians,[17] Ephesians, the Pastoral Epistles (i.e., 1 and 2 Timothy and Titus), and 1 Peter. Acts also belongs to the same period. These writings were all written somewhere between 70 and 105. Claiming to be by apostolic authors, they sought to adjust the apostolic teaching to the changed conditions of the sub-apostolic age. The original witnesses were dying out, the church was obviously here to stay, the second coming was indefinitely delayed. Moreover, the church was faced by the threat of false teaching of the kind which goes by the name of gnosticism.[18] The church's response to this new situation was to develop its organization, and to adapt its ways to the surrounding society. In this period there was great emphasis on law and order in family and social life. The emphasis which we have already seen in the genuine Paul on subordination of women (1 Cor 11), qualified though it was by Paul's sense of the newness of life under the gospel, was developed without Paul's corresponding emphasis on the newness. Thus we get a series of household codes in which wives are taught to be subject to their husbands (Col 3:18ff; Eph 5:21ff; Ti 2:1 - 10ff). In addition it was in this period that the first evidence for ordination occurs (1 Tm 1:18; 4:14; 2 Tm 1:14; Ti 1:5; cf. Acts 14:23). This ordained ministry consisted of people like Timothy and Titus ("apostolic men" as Bishop Gore called them), and of bishop-presbyters (the titles appear to be interchangeable in the Pastorals and Acts),[19] and of deacons. There were also widows who provided only auxiliary services. The ministry of the Word was performed by presbyter-bishops, i.e. only by men, and women were expressly forbidden to speak in church:

> Let a woman learn in silence with all submissiveness. I permit no woman to teach or to have authority over men; she is to keep silent. For Adam was formed first, then Eve; and Adam was not deceived, but the woman was deceived and became a transgressor.   — 1 Tm 2:11 - 14

We have already suggested that this was written by the same hand who interpolated 1 Cor 14:34 - 36 (see above). Once again, recourse is had to the Genesis creation stories to justify the subordination of women. This later writer, though a member of the Pauline school, has dropped one side of his master's teaching (1 Cor 11:5; Gal 3:28) and developed only the other (1 Cor 11:3, 7 - 8). As a result the freedom which Paul had allowed for the ministries of women prophets in Corinth, of Euodia and Syntyche at Philippi, of Prisca and Phoebe and others, had to be surrendered to the needs of a later day. What then happened to Paul's eschatological woman? She was sacrificed to the needs of consolidation, of accommodation to the mores of contemporary society, to the threat of gnosticism. The answer to our question is that Paul's eschatological woman had probably become a gnostic!

What does this latest period of the New Testament teach us then? Not that the rules it lays down are valid for all time. As a matter of fact, the ministry continued to adapt itself to later needs. In the second century "monepiscopacy" (a single bishop in each central city church) replaced the presbyter-bishops of the Pastorals and Acts. Adaptation and flexibility were the keynotes of ministry in the New Testament period. Its regulations are nowhere prescriptive for all time. If in Paul's churches women were allowed to exercise a full ministry of the word (and perhaps even of sacrament), though under a single restriction of being veiled, and if in the sub-apostolic age women were silenced; if too in Paul's churches there was no ordination, and if by the time there was ordination there was no ministry of women apart from the widows, the New Testament says to us that the church is free to adapt its ministry to the needs of the age. The two motives that led to the restriction of the ministry of women — that society accepted the principle of woman's subordination and that women were too often prone to the temptation of gnosticism, no longer obtain today. If women today are as well educated as men and have the same place in society, if too there is no reason to suspect that women, more than men, will be prone to false teaching, then, so far as the New Testament is concerned, there is absolutely no reason why the full ordained ministry should be denied to women. In fact, we should be able today to implement Gal 3:28 as has not been possible since Paul.

NOTES

1 Mk 1:16 - 20 par.; 2:13 - 14 par.; Mt 8:19 - 22 par.

2 Mt 19:28; cf Lk 22:28 - 30. For the authenticity of this saying, which has been questioned, see R. H. Fuller, THE FOUNDATIONS OF NEW TESTAMENT CHRISTOLOGY (N.Y.: Scribners, 1965), pp. 123 - 24.

3 There are variations in the lists of the Twelve, but the names are invariably male: Mk 3:16 - 19 par., Acts 1:13 - 14.

4 See e.g., Oscar Cullman, CHRIST AND TIME (Philadelphia: Westminster, 1964).

5 The most famous instance of this view is in Albert Schweitzer's QUEST OF THE HISTORICAL JESUS (London: Black, 1910), pp. 368 - 69.

6 The confusion is straightened out by Raymond E. Brown, S.S., THE GOSPEL ACCORDING TO JOHN (Garden City, N.Y.: Doubleday, 1966), pp. 449 - 54.

7 For the nucleus of historical tradition enshrined in the Marcan story of the empty tomb see R. H. Fuller, THE FORMATION OF THE RESURRECTION NARRATIVES (N.Y.: Macmillan, 1971), pp. 52 - 57.

8 Some will be troubled by Paul's subordinationist Christology here. That is however not our present concern. Suffice it to say that Paul wrote at a very early stage in the development of Christology and was uninhibited about subordinationist statements which later would have seemed unorthodox. See also 1 Cor 15:28 for another subordinationist statement in a different connection.

9 ". . . this infection of nature doth remain, yea in them that are regenerated." Article IX.

10 See any Old Testament Introduction or Commentary on Genesis. See e.g., Charles M. Laymon (ed.), THE INTERPRETERS' ONE-VOLUME COMMENTARY ON THE BIBLE (Nashville: Abingdon, 1971), pp. i - 3.

11 E. g., 1 Cor 3:5. "Deaconess" is probably an anachronism in Rom 16:1.

12 See Burton Scott Easton, THE PASTORAL EPISTLES (New York: Scribners, 1947), p. 226.

13 See the remarkable collection of essays by French Roman Catholic scholars, Jean Delorme (ed.), LE MINISTERE ET LES MINISTERES SELON LE NOVEAU TESTAMENT (Paris: Seuil, 1973).

14 Hans von Campenhausen, ECCLESIASTICAL AUTHORITY AND SPIRITUAL POWER IN THE CHURCH OF THE FIRST THREE CENTURIES (Stanford, CA.: Stanford University, 1969).

15 This means that Acts 14:23, while good evidence for what went on in Luke's church, is an anachronism so far as Paul is concerned (so Easton). Ordination expresses two things: divine appointment and ecclesial recognition. These things were expressed differently during the Apostolic Age.

16 Henri Denis and Jean Delorme in Delorme, *op. cit.,* 506.

17 How many would regard Colossians as Pauline? For our purposes this question does not matter, since, while Col is evidence for a subordinationist view of women (testified also in the Pauline homologoumena), it offers no evidence for women in the ministry, pro or con.

18 More properly one should speak of "gnosis" in this period. Gnosis means a tendency of thought which antedates the great gnostic systems of the second century, to which the name gnosticism should properly be confined.

19 This is clear in Acts: compare Acts 20:17 with 20:28, which speaks of the same group as "elders" (Greek: *presbyteroi*) and "guardians" (RSV; Greek: *episcopoi* = bishops).

2 The Authority of the Ministry

Frederick H. Borsch

— I —

Aspects of the debate regarding the rightness of opening all orders of the ordained ministry to women have been concerned with the issue of the proper exercise of proper authority. Is it legitimate and is it fitting that the authority pertaining to the offices of bishop and priest be exercised by a person who is female? Can a woman really do this in an effective and legitimate manner in and for a branch of the catholic church? One more than suspects that, even when such questions are not brought explicitly into the debate, they lurk behind other arguments, acting as specters of implicit doubt.

When best formulated, this questioning has nothing to do with the issue of whether women actually have the ability to carry out the duties and responsibilities of these offices. One presumes that in a time when women have been running governments and companies, working above, below and alongside of men, we are not asking whether there are women who can wisely and skillfully lead diocesan councils and vestry meetings, preach, manage budgets and say expressively the words of blessing, formal absolution and eucharistic consecration. The significant question is whether it is right and effective in and for the church that women should do these things — especially whether they should have authority to be stewards of the Word and the

sacraments. Are there biblical, theological or psychological reasons why it is necessary or at least best that only men bear this
authority of stewardship? In other words, the real question con-
centrates attention on a different kind of authority than is commonly understood as authority in the halls of government,
schools and business.[1]

I intend here to focus on a particular and essential character
of the authority of Christian ministry, especially as it is presented
in the New Testament. Because of this focus, the study can be
neither comprehensive nor definitive. A number of important
issues will be left aside. What we will attempt to accomplish is
to show that this particular character is of the essence of the
authority of all Christian ministry — not the least the ordained
ministry; that is, the authority of ministry becomes unrecognizable as true Christian authority without this character. It will
then be asked whether this essential character should be viewed
as pertaining especially or necessarily to male human beings.

— II —

From its inception the Christian community has rightly
understood its ministry as an extension of that of Jesus. All
ministry takes place as a function of the body of Christ serving
in the world, and all Christians are to see themselves as "am-
bassadors of Christ" (2 Cor 5:20). Although the members of
the body are many and the gifts of the Spirit diverse, there is
a fundamental Christ-likeness which is to characterize Christian
living.[2] All ministry and all priesthood are regarded as being
enacted in the imitation of Christ.[3]

Paul gives insight into a vital property of true discipleship
when he calls upon Jesus' followers to,

> Have this mind among yourselves, which you have in
> Christ Jesus, who, though he was in the form of God,
> did not count equality with God a thing to be grasped,
> but emptied himself, taking the form of a servant.[4]

It is indeed through this humbling of himself — especially to
the obedience of his death — that Jesus' authority of Lordship
("the name which is above every name") is bestowed upon him
by God, "that at the name of Jesus every knee should bow"
(Phil 2:9 - 10). The authority of God made known in Christ is
an authority which posts at its heart the cross of Calvary. The

hands by which humankind is to be judged are known by Christians to have holes in their palms.

This understaning also forms one of the basic motifs of the Epistle to the Hebrews. Jesus is "crowned with glory and honor because of the suffering of death" (2:9). Because he is "made like his brethren in every respect", he is able to "become a merciful and faithful high priest." In that "he himself has suffered and been tempted, he is able to help those who are tempted" (2:17 - 18). Christ did not exalt himself to be high priest. Rather "was it granted by God," for, "although he was Son, he learned obedience through what he suffered." So was he "named high priest by God" (5:5, 8 - 10).

The theme is given its full resonance through the memory of Jesus' ministry as it is presented by the evangelists. Not only is he rememberd as having told stories about the meaning of true humility and the servant character of leadership, but he is seen standing in and behind his words — enacting his own parables. At the Last Supper, Jesus presides as the one who gives of his very life "for many" (Mk 14:24 = Mt 26:28). In the fourth gospel, the Lord rises from the table to wash his disciples' feet, wiping them with a towel with which he had girded himself. "I have given you an example, that you also should do as I have done to you" (Jn 13:15).

Yet repeatedly the disciples do not understand the nature of Jesus' authority. They wish to interpret it in terms of rights and privileges and ask that they may receive special positions of honor. Jesus admonishes them:

> You know that those who are supposd to rule over the Gentiles lord it over them. But it shall not be so among you; but whoever would be great among you must be your servant, and whoever would be first among you must be slave of all. For the Son of man also came not to be served but to serve. (Mk 10:42 - 45)

This is a lesson that is never completely learned by Christians, and time and time again, throughout church history and in our own lives, it is doubted or dealt with by rationalization. Paul finds the same problem cropping up in the Corinthian community. By the standards of worldly wisdom, the power of the cross seems no power at all.[5] There is an aspect of each one of us which, together with those first onlookers, stands watching Jesus being crucified and taunts, "If you are the Son of God, come down from the cross." "Let him come down now from the cross, and we will believe in him" (Mt 27:40, 42).

It would be far easier to worship God if he demanded that we serve him. Instead, he serves us, and in so doing calls us to serve each other. Indeed this motif of communal ministry to *one another* resounds through the New Testament and is intended to echo in the different persons of the disciples as they seek to let the spirit of Jesus be manifeted in their own lives. "Wash one another's feet" (Jn 13:14); "forbear and forgive one another" (Col 3:13); "comfort one another and build each other up" (1 Thes 5:11); "Love one another; just as I have loved you, you also are to love one another" (Jn 13:34); "serve one another" (Gal 5:13); "teach and admonish one another" (Col 3:16); "bear one another's burdens" (Gal 6:2); "be at peace one with another" (1 Thes 5:13); "God himself lives within us if we love one another" (1 Jn 4:12).

By means of the narrative of his testing by the devil, the Gospels dramatize Jesus' own temptations to misconstrue the character of his ministry. The story of his denial of the three temptations to demonstrate the authority of his messiahhip (by means of supplying immediate needs, dominating in terms of worldly power or dragooning faith through miraculous activities) is set forth as a way of indicating his awareness of what the uses of power can do to corrupt those who wield it, and their causes. Especially it is understood that spiritual and moral power is the strongest and most readily corruptible power of all.[6] It can only be used for the benefit of others by those who have learned the meaning of servanthood.

In Christian theology the ministry of the historical Jesus is understood as an exemplification of God's own eternal will and character. "No one has ever seen God; but God's only Son, he who is nearest to the Father's heart, he has made him known" (Jn 1:18). Jesus is for Christians a kind of aperture through which insights into the divine presence can be perceived, revealing that God is always willing to give and share of himself. In and through Jesus there is realized the possibility that one of humankind's repeated myth dreams has become a reality. The great king himself comes to share in the life of his people. He rules not from above but among and within, through the offering of his love.

— III —

Given this understanding of the significance of Jesus to the Christian community, it is hardly surprising that a word often used of disciples in the New Testament is servant. Disciples are servants of God and of Jesus and of one another in the body of Christ. As Jesus had been among them "as one who serves" (Lk 22:27), so a follower like Paul, though free from all, makes himself "a servant to everyone to win over as many as possible" (1 Cor 9:19). Paul understands that his authority in Christ is best manifested when he presents himself as servant to those whom he calls to faith in Jesus. This interpretation of the disciples' role has made its way into the English language in one form though the very word minister, for a minister (from the Latin word for servant or assistant) has a minor role: service to others.

At their baptism, all Christians are commissioned to be such ministers and to "confess the faith of Christ crucified, proclaim his resurrection, and share with us in his eternal priesthood."[7] Every disciple is to signify in and for the body of Christ and to the world the character of servanthood which is so vital an aspect of all Christian ministry conducted in the imitation of Christ.

That which is so significant for all Christian ministry must be recognized as essential to the ordained ministry. "The Canterbury Statement" — the agreed-upon statement on the ministry drafted by representative Roman Catholic and Anglican theologians — speaks of the ordained person as a necessary focus of leadership and unity. It continues: "In the New Testament a variety of images is used to describe the functions of this minister. He is servant, both of Christ and of the Church."[8] By giving it a primary position, this statement rightly stresses the necessary character of servanthood for those who are to act as foci for the Christian witness and community. It is our argument that — just as this character distinguished the authority of Jesus as Lord and Christ and was commended to his disciples by Word and enacted parables — so it must be understood as of the essence of the exercise of all genuinely Christian authority. This is not to attribute the efficacy of particular sacramental acts to the virtues of the ordained person or to suggest that these acts are not efficacious when performed by those who do not exemplify servanthood in their lives. But it is to say that the practice of ministry — and specifically the exercise of its authority — becomes unrecognizable as Christian (in the imitation of Christ) when it is done by those who do not know themselves to be servants.

This awareness can be given special emphasis in every office of the ordained ministry. The very name deacon derives from the Greek word regularly translated as servant. Although from the inception of the office deacons have been understood to have a variety of duties, their first and chief responsibility has been to render service — oftentimes menial — to the larger community. They are authorized to act as servants; they have the authority to carry out certain tasks, in some cases felt to be best reserved to those with training and a calling, for and on behalf of the body of Christ.

In the All Saints' Chapel of the Church Divinity School of the Pacific there is a stained glass window depicting the traditional figure of Christ the King as a royal priest. Yet underneath his chasuble there is clearly visible the dalmatic, the garment symbolizing his work as deacon to his people. It is a proper understanding of the entire ordained ministry that, though other responsibilities may be added, the office of deacon continues to be an aspect of all other offices.

There is a sense in which all other offices should be viewed as an intensification of the role of a deacon. The bishop is a locus of meaning for all Christian ministry but particularly the ordained ministry. This person is to serve the priests and deacons in special roles. For and on behalf of others the bishop is to be a steward of Word and sacraments, having been asked to bear the authority necessary for this work. Together with other bishops this individual is given a special responsibility as a preserver and proclaimer of the Christian faith and for the sacrament of ordination which commissions others to act for the community in sacramental roles. The episcopal authority extends from Jesus through his body, the community of Christian witness. The bishop is a servant to the servants of God.

The priest acts as a focal point for ministry in local Christian communities. For and on behalf of others the priest takes on the responsibilities of being a steward of the Word and sacraments. The authority to serve as priest is understood to come from the Lord through his body and through the bishop acting for Christ and Christ's body. But once more, as the authority given by Jesus, it is by its character of servanthood that it will most clearly be known, and through this same character that it is to help win the hearts of men and women to follow the one who best showed what it means to serve rather than to be served.

With these understandings in mind, it is appropriate that our greatest concerns with the rightful exercise of Christian authority should have at least as much to do with issues involving its servant character as with other definitions or descriptions of legitimacy. So often in the life of the church it is forms of clericalism — the misapprehension and misuse of the authority of ordained persons — which does the greatest damage to the practice of the ordained ministry and all ministry.[9] How easily is the authority of the ordained ministry twisted about so as to cause lay persons to be understood as the servants of the ordained clergy rather than the clergy as those specially chosen to enact particular forms of service for the sake of the body.

— IV —

The subject of the authority of the ministry is complex and cannot be fully dealt with under any one category. We have attempted, however, to indicate how fundamental and crucial to the exercise of ministerial authority is the character of servanthood. It is by this character that this authority can be recognized as Christian. The next question we are led to ask is whether there is anything about this character of servanthood which — on biblical, theological, psychological or other grounds — pertains exclusively or predominantly to either the male or female sex.

The argument might be made that servanthood is more characteristically female than male. Historically, in many societies, women have been thought of, and more importantly, sometimes have thought of themselves, predominantly in servant-like roles. Very often their authority as mothers and wives has stemmed from the essential service they offered. The gift which women will bring to the ordained ministry — through the experience of this tradition — will be of great benefit in reshaping the face of more aggressive models of authority.

It is of significance also to recognize how female imagery for God and Jesus finds expression in the Judeo-Christian tradition when the idea of loving service and sacrifice comes to the fore. The Lord God, acting to save the people of Israel, "will cry out like a woman in travail" (Is 42:14). When it is said that the Lord has forgotten Zion, the prophet asks rhetorically, "Can a woman forget her suckling child, that she should have no compassion on the son of her womb?" (Is 49:15). Thus says the Lord, "As one whom his mother comforts, so I will comfort you" (Is 66:13). Jesus cries out in anguish to the holy city of his people: "O Jerusalem, Jerusalem, . . . How often would I have gathered your children together as a hen gathers her brood under her wings and you would not!" (Lk 13:34 = Mt 23:37).

What has been called the earliest Christian hymnbook, THE ODES OF SOLOMON, speaks with mixed imagery of the fulness of God the Father's breasts and how the female Holy Spirit gives of this milk for the chosen.[10] Julian of Norwich, one of the great mystical writers of the Anglican tradition, not infrequently pictures God and Jesus in the language of maternal imagery:

> The human mother will suckle her child with her own milk, but our beloved Mother, Jesus, feeds us with himself, and with most tender courtesy, does it by means of the Blessed Sacrament, the precious food of all true life . . . The human mother may put her child tenderly to her breast, but our tender Mother Jesus simply leads us into his blessed breast, through his open side, and there gives us a glimpse of the Godhead and heavenly joy, the inner certainty of eternal bliss.[11]

The quotations could be extended, but it is in fact not our concern to attempt to demonstrate that the character of servanthood and of sacrificial love belongs in some predominant manner to either sex. Fathers, sons and husbands as well as male friends can act as loving servants too. We take it to be Julian's point that the imagery used of self-offering and giving, while not excluding sexuality, reaches beyond the lineaments of maleness and femaleness to include the wholeness of humanity. Similarly we maintain that the unique property of the authority of Christian ministry, which derives from its character of servanthood, should be understood to be manifested through our humanity — as God has chosen to do through incarnation — and pertains in no particularistic manner to either sex.

This is not to say that sexual nature makes no difference. One has little doubt but that women acting as priests and bishops will add new dimensions to our understanding of the practice of ordained ministry and of the exercise of its authority. It can be argued that their presence may be catalytic for one of the periodic reformations which the ministry needs regularly to undergo. Yet even this consideration is but secondary to our main point:

the authority of the ordained ministry, insofar as it derives from the essential and vital character of servanthood, can very well be exercised by women.

— V —

One point bears stressing: the Christian servanthood we understand here is born in strength and not impotence. Among its properties are the humility of spirit, meekness, mercifulness, and desire to be a peacemaker of which we hear Jesus speaking in the Sermon on the Mount. Yet it is in conjunction with the qualities and not in distinction from them that the servant may also need to act as prophet, as one who hungers and thirsts after righteousness (Mt 5:6).

Jesus can drive the money changers from the temple because he comes as one who serves. The same Mary who is presented to us as the lowly handmaiden and humble mother can proclaim God's justice in ringing words.

He has shown strength with his arm,
He has scattered the proud in the imagination of their hearts,
He has put down the mighty from their seat,
and has exalted the humble and meek. (Lk 1:51 - 2)

The authority which God gives into the hands of his servants, though it may sometimes appear like other forms of human authority, has a very different and sometimes surprising basis. Many of us keep thinking it ought to work some other way. Like Jesus' disciples we prefer to call down fire from heaven rather than to follow him to Jerusalem (Lk 9:51 - 6). We choose to employ anger in our own causes rather than to speak of the healing justice of God which challenges and seeks to liberate all persons. (So does anger uncontrolled by the spirit of servanthood turn righteousness into self-righteouness.) Often it is much easier to try to maneuver people by the strings of their guilt — as do so many would-be reformers — rather than to give them the acceptance and caring which can really make them free to change.

Of course this is true of us. We are only beginners, people barely starting to grow toward "the measure of the stature of the fulness of Christ" (Eph 4:13). Yet we are the very same people for whom the strength of servanthood begins to become a possibility. It is our acceptance and forgiveness by God in Jesus which enables us to know that we are loved. In the power of that love we are made love*able* — able to love ourselves and so able to love our neighbors as ourselves. We are commissioned to offer service and challenge with the authority of a love which seeks never to dominate but to share the power of acceptance and forgiveness with others.

In that commission and authority all human persons may share. Here we find reason to believe that women as well as men can participate in the particular responsibilities of servant authority which pertain to the ordained ministry. Thus in this area of concern, as in others, we feel compelled to ask the same question as was forced upon the first evangelists: can the good news of and about Jesus be proclaimed in variant cultural conditions and in the context of understandings of reality different from those in which it was first preached? The early disciples' answer to that question is written all over the pages of the New Testament. As participants in a faith more oriented toward the future than the past, they were made to learn how they could risk giving up all that was not essential to the gospel in order to preach and practice its fundamental beliefs in new ways among new peoples. We should hardly be surprised to discover that similar tasks and opportunities are ours.

NOTES

1 This understanding is forcefully stated by the Roman Catholic theologian George Tavard, who in his book WOMEN IN CHRISTIAN TRADITION (Notre Dame: Univ. of Notre Dame Press, 1974) argues for the ordination of women to all offices in the Church: "Those who build their case for women priests or women ministers on the basis of feminine emancipation in society can never reach a persuasive conclusion. For we are not at this point dealing with society, but with the Church; and we should not base our views on political and social convenience and opportunity, but on the Gospel and the dynamics of the coming Kingdom. Neither here or anywhere else should the Church take the world as its norm." (p. 219). While agreeing with Tavard's important insight, we would nevertheless not wish in any sense to exclude the possibility that the Holy Spirit is in "the world" acting to bring about human liberation. Indeed, there is much in the Gospels, Paul and the Bible generally that— sometimes quite apart from "church activities" — may have permeated our societies, helping to incite a hope reaching toward new understandings of freedom and justice. In this sense the Church ought to be prepared also to learn from the Holy Spirit acting beyond any visible delineations of the Church.

2 See 1 Cor 12 where Paul discusses how the different gifts of ministry are inspired by the same Spirit, Lord and God.

3 This is expressed most forcefully for many Christians by Jesus' bidding, "If

any one would come after me, let him deny himself and take up his cross and follow me." Mk 8:34. Similarly Mt 10:38, 16:24, and Lk 9:23, 14:27. See also Jn 12:26, "If any one serves me, he must follow me; and where I am, there shall my servant be also."

4 Phil 2:5 - 7. Two of the Greek words most frequently translated as "servant" in the New Testament and used to characterize Christian discipleship are *doulos* and *diakonos. Doulos,* which is used in this passage from Philippians, is also translated as "slave." Although careful distinctions between the two words were not kept, *doulos* can be employed to contrast slaves to masters and free men. It is often used to stress dependence. *Diakonos* carries more the connotation of a helper or assistant without implying that the individual is in a situation of total subservience. The *doulos* would be thought to have a lesser degree of freedom than the *diakonos,* but *doulos* is given a special meaning in Christian usage, since Jesus or his disciple is said freely to choose this status.

5 See 1 Cor 1:18 - 31.

6 The story is found in Mt 4:1 - 11 and Lk 4:1 - 13. We here suggest that the Lucan version, which puts as the last and greatest temptation that of throwing oneself down from the pinnacle of the temple, is the more dramatic in psychological and spiritual terms.

7 "Holy Baptism" in Authorized Services 1973 (N.Y.: The Church Hymnal Corp., 1973), p. 12.

8 "The Canterbury Statement" has been reprinted in a number of places. It is found conveniently in *The Anglican Theological Review,* LVII/1, 1975. Pp. 95 - 100. The report of a colloquium reflecting on the statement precedes it. The quotation is from p. 97 of this edition of the statement.

9 This understanding of the dangers of clericalism on the parts of both men and women clergy is well stated by Alda Marsh in "Sexism in the Church: A Case for Listening to 'The Other Woman'." *A Journal of Ministry in Higher Education* (Winter, 1974), pp. 4 - 12.

10 J. H. Charlesworth (ed.) *The Odes of Solomon* (London: Oxford U.P., 1973), 19.1 - 4; see also *Ode* 8.14.

11 Julian of Norwich, REVELATIONS OF DIVINE LOVE (trans. and ed., Clifton Walters. Baltimore: Penguin, 1966) p. 170. The passage is quoted by E. L. McLaughlin, "The Church Past: Does it Hold a Future for Women?" *The Anglican Theological Review* (LVII/1, 1975), p. 49.

3 Women in the Early Church:

A Problem of Perspective

Lloyd G. Patterson

A preliminary piece of evidence

One of the more striking of the so-called "praying figures," *orantes,* found at early Christian burial sites is a third century (?) painting on a wall of the Priscillian catacomb at Rome.[1] In many respects, the figure follows the conventions governing this form of early Christian art. The person there interred is shown standing with arms upraised, as that person once stood by virtue of baptism in the eucharistic meeting on the Lord's Day and will stand with the full assembly of God's people at the Last Day. Thus it presents that person in true Christian identity.[2]

What gives this figure its particular grandeur is the way in which the motif of light, *locus lucis,* one of the conventional features of an *orans,* is introduced. In this case, the face and upstretched hands are bathed in light, so that the figure itself reflects back to the visitor the light of Christ beginning to be manifest in the darkness of this world.

Other things which a modern visitor might like to know are obscure. The identity of the person depicted, his or her sex, his or her special function in the Church, are hard to determine. In this case, there is no inscription of the sort which is often added to an *orans.* Surrounding scenes, as well as a ceremonial scarf falling across the head to the shoulders, may identify the person as a virgin veiled. Yet the treatment of the hair, often the only pictorial indication of sex, seems to me at least to suggest that the person is male. Dress is no help. The figure wears, over the usual white tunic, an overcoat of Dalmatian cut, with sleeves, rather than one of the poncho sort, *paenula*, more common in the period. But these garments were worn by pagans as well as Christians, by men as well as women, of whatever calling in the Church, throughout the period.

The evidence suggests that it is a male figure. But it is a matter of conjecture, precisely because the conventions governing this form of early Christian art are concerned with other things. What these conventions do, and in this case do admirably, is to show the true identity of the person as one whose participation in the Christian community is a foretaste of participation in the redeemed community of God. Other matters were, fortunately or unfortunately, of less interest to the artist than to the modern visitor to the site.

The problem of perspectives

The Priscillian *orans* may help to explain the purpose of these remarks.

It is plainly impossible to write briefly about the place of women in the first three or four centuries of the Christian movement. This period saw the movement spread through and beyond Judaism into the vast reaches of the Graeco-Roman society, witnessed its persecutions at the hands of the imperial government and its eventual acceptance as the official cultus of the state, and its many and various attempts to interpret itself in the light of the intellectual world of the time. The historical panorama is extensive, Christian practice and thought diverse, the evidence remaining scattered and difficult of generalization. Efforts to deal with the subject are numerous. But they constitute a literature more extensive than definitive, to which it is almost literally painful to contemplate adding a few more pages.

The danger of beginning with this literature itself lies in the fact that it almost inevitably approaches early Christian evidence with modern issues in mind. This is particularly true when it asks why women were not admitted to holy orders — at least to the orders of presbyter and bishop — in the period. It is also true when it goes farther afield to ask how early Christians viewed sexuality, personal identity, and other matters on which the evidence is far more difficult to interpret. Periodically, the attitude of the writer informs the answers which the evidence is thought to give, with the result that the early centuries turn out either to have established important criteria for Christian life or to have deviated from the Gospel under the influence of inherited social customs, the influence of pagan philosophy, or some other misfortune, depending on where the writer stands on modern issues.[3]

The point is that this literature, like the modern visitor to the Priscillian *orans*, is sorely tempted to ask questions which the evidence will not anwer, failing all the while to absorb what the evidence actually has to say. This has, of course, been the difficulty with much writing on the early Church since the age of Charlemagne, whenever pressing contemporary issues have led us to review how things came to be as they are, whether good or bad. What seems hardest to get at is what the early Church, let speak for itself, might have to say in its own way about matters of contemporary interest.

The problem is thus one of perspectives — not of discovering something new so much as of putting what is already known in its own perspective rather than ours. That is no easy problem to solve; but it is one that can at least be raised, and then left to the consideration of the reader.

Church in early Christianity

The first subject to be considered is our *orans* itself. The figure, standing with upraised arms, reflecting back light to the visitor, identifies the person interred there as a member of the Church, *ecclesia,* the "assembling" of a redeemed humanity which God has begun to make through the death and resurrection of Christ.

No aspect of early Christianity — liturgical, ethical, or theological — can be seriously studied where this fundamental sense of what it means to be a Christian is left out of account. It is assumed more often than spelled out in references to the baptismal and eucharistic meetings, or when the style of life required of those who take the name Christian is discussed, or where the proclamation of God's work in Christ is interpreted in the light of contemporary thought.[4]

But Church always stands opposed to World, *cosmos,* in

early Christianity. To be part of redeemed humanity-to-come is to be such in the midst of presently unredeemed humanity. To be part of "the age to come" is to be that in the midst of "the present age", to live in an alien environment, to expect opposition from the powers which, however fruitlessly, seek to thwart the power of God. It is to live now, literally or figuratively, a life of "martyrdom", of witness to belief that the new life in Christ will be triumphant over the old life of the world.

In its tendency to oppose church and world, early Christianity was the inheritor of many strands of later Jewish thought, which from the Maccabean period onward were given concrete form in the notion of an inevitable conflict between the people of God and the political powers which opposed them. Eventually, of course, the Roman *imperium,* with its slowly evolving policy of opposition to the Christian movement, came to be regarded as the final manifestation of these powers. Indeed, even after the persecutions ceased and the imperial and other high offices were occupied by Christians, a sense of hostility between the church and the world represented in the *imperium* remained a conscious factor in Christian thinking. It was only when that situation had in some psychological sense become "past", perhaps not until the age of Charlemagne, that a vision of a Christian Empire could arise to the imagination as a heritage to be recovered rather than an anomaly to be lived with.

We cannot expect early Christians, thinking in this way, to approach any aspect of the problem of "liberation" in quite the way we do. Neither can we expect them to associate self-fulfillment with the given social structures in anything like the the way Christians have come to do because of the experience of the church's actual involvement with those structures in the so-called era of Christendom and its aftermath. By our standards their perceptions seem severely limited when they exhort one another to avoid sexual license, elaborate clothing, the luxuries of the baths, or the exitements and the pagan associations of the spectacles, the theater, and the literary classics. And the same is true of the modest efforts at the betterment of the human condition undertaken by those in positions of leadership in the period after the persecutions. From their own perspective, however, what was chiefly at stake was the integrity of the new life they were called to live in the midst of the old. Theirs was a very positive — a positively negative — attitude toward a number of aspects of the old life, what we would class as social conventions or even legal prescriptions. They thought these conventions and prescriptions were in the process of being abrogated by a power greater than the powers responsible for them.

It is in this light that we must read Paul's much discussed statement that in Christ there is "neither Jew nor Greek, slave nor free, male nor female" (Gal 3:28). Paul is not here enunciating an ideal to be achieved in the church — much less in the world — but saying something about the manifestation of the new life in the midst of the old in the congregations with which he is familiar. Plainly, he is also talking about what we might assume, from our perspective, to be an alternative to the conventions and prescriptions of paganism and Judaism. But in fact he is speaking from a perspective so different from ours that it is better to withhold judgment until we have said something about what he — and his successors — quite concretely meant by such statements.

Women in the church in early Christianity

We can use our *orans* once again to introduce the question of what the abrogation of "male and female" meant in early Christianity. The question of the sex of the person interred would not arise if we did not know from any number of sources that women as well as men underwent baptism and took part in the eucharistic meetings on the Lord's Day. Centuries of familiarity with the practice, as well as loss of touch with the meaning attached to the "assembling" of the people of God for what we now tend to undervalue as mere liturgical events, may lead us to think of it as less significant than it is. Set in contrast to the synagogue, where an assembly capable of giving thanks to God is defined by the presence of circumcised males, the church is a visual proof that the distinction of "male and female" is abrogated in Christ. It may seem to us merely a matter of who could "go to Church", but the early Christians did not regard it so. It is a question of perspectives again.

Other evidence, scattered and spotty though it may be, helps to fill out the picture. Paul sends greetings to women as well as men in his letters. Women as well as men were celebrated for their martyrdom, the *passio* of Perpetua and her companions being perhaps the best known of many accounts in circulation. The Christian women of Rome stand out in successive generations, not merely the martyrs in considerable number, but such persons as the Flora whom Ptolemy sought to convert to Valentian Gnosis, as those who befriended Athanasius during his exile, and as the household with which Jerome corresponded regarding the superiority of eastern ascetic practices. Then, too, in Asia Minor there is the community of ascetic women for which Methodius wrote his *Symposium,* his most elaborate exposition of the place of the ascetic life in the plan of salvation. And one must at least mention the theological insights attributed to Macrina by her brother Gregory of Nyssa, and to Monica by her son Augustine of Hippo.[5]

It is easy to notice the contradictory evidence that the social conventions which assigned to women a subordinate place in the family and in public life continued to be reflected in the life of the church, and are supported by theological argument. Leaving aside for the moment the problem of women in the "ministry", we should note that women are said to be subject to their husbands and to leave the running of affairs to men because of their weaknesses, their creation from the rib of Adam (Gn 2:21), and the guilt which falls on them as descendants of Eve. Moreover, on any statistical view of the evidence, women do not appear in great numbers among the notable figures of the period, doubtless because of the influence of inherited custom if not of the theological arguments made in support of it.[6]

And then, again, looking at the period from a modern point of view, it may well seem that the attitude toward marriage is such that the sexuality of the female in particular is regarded as a liability to her being truly human. In fact the women celebrated in the early Christian evidence — leaving the martyrs on one side — are ascetics.

Here, however, we confront a much more complicated aspect of early Christianity, which is the fact that it owed much to its origin among those movements within Judaism which not only expected hostility from the world but sought to demonstrate their freedom from it by embracing continence (*encrateia*). That many primitive Christian communities were committed to continence in this sense, at least in principle, is clear from the Pauline letters and other writings from the gentile wing of the movement no less than from the newly appreciated Jewish-Christian and proto-gnostic writings.[7] Such an attitude, of course, does not involve the judgment that sexuality is evil; but the defense of marriage mounted by the Alexandrian and Cappadocian theologians against a developed Gnosticism convinced of the evil character of the physical creation and against pagan philosophical tradition unconvinced of the desirability of embodied existence altogether, goes no further than saying that it is a controlled way by means of which the increase of humanity to its perfection is to be achieved by procreation. The *encratitic* ideal continued even in non-gnostic circles. It underlies the concern of the early Christian communities for the support of virgins and widows (persons most likely to be forced to marry in the prevailing circumstances), and forms the basis of the great fascination with the ascetic life which followed the end of the persecutions.

The early Christians adopted the attitude toward women which it inherited, and even defended it, as among the characteristics of fallen humanity. But at the same time, they acknowledged that this attitude was transformed in Christ. There is certainly a good deal of tension to be found in the evidence on this point. But the fact is that women are not celebrated as Christians because they fall easily into special roles set aside for women, as in the pagan cults or in the Jewish family, but because they do the things which every Christian may be celebrated for doing. In the context of that time this fact looms much larger than it does in ours.

On the subject of the *encratitic* tendency of early Christianity we are in a much more complicated area. It is obvious from the evidence that sexuality is simply not regarded as so closely related to personal identity as we take it to be as a result of a series of developments from the early Middle Ages to the work of Freud and his successors. Rightly or wrongly, the abandonment of marriage is seen as a means of transcending the social restrictions and of avoiding the passionate aspect of procreation — or rather of witnessing to the fact that they are transcended in Christ — in a way that is foreign to our thinking. But it remains to be shown that the full range of attributes which make up what we describe as "selfhood" is not taken into account.

Perhaps it can be said that the evidence most easily falls together if we say that for early Christians the abrogation of the distinction of "male and female" in Christ is most clearly manifest, apart from the liturgical meetings themselves, in the ways in which men and women act "beyond" the social structures of the fallen world. This will be highly unsatisfactory both to the proponents of a liberation theology and to those who think that the social patterns of the early Christian period are applicable to the circumstances of the present. It is, however, a matter of a perspective so different from ours that it is hard to render an immediate judgment upon it.

Women in the "ministry" of the church in early Christianity

We come, now, to the place of women as deacons, presbyters and bishops, or in what we now call the "ministry" of the church, the subject of considerable contemporary interest and of no little confusion and controversy at that time.

There is no question that women functioned with men as deacons throughout the period, caring for needy members of the congregations, helping candidates during the baptismal liturgy, and certainly in many places reading scriptures and administering the communion at the eucharist. There is, however, a good deal of evidence of conscious opposition, within the "Catholic" communities from the latter part of the second century on, to women functioning among the presbyters on whom the administration of the affairs of the congregations fell. And there is no evidence from the episcopal lists of the same communities that they functioned as bishops, those on whom by that time the main burden of teaching and of presiding at the baptismal and eucharistic meetings had fallen.

In the writings of the time it can be noticed that no real rationale is offered for any of these offices — it is left to the common assumptions of the time — except in the case of the defense of the episcopacy as the guarantee of the continuity of the apostolic preaching and of the unity of the church.[8] And to this can be added the more or less obvious point that inherited convention more or less dictated who would occupy them. Thus women no less than men might be expected to function as deacons in this peculiarly Christian office, since there were women as well as men who needed its ministrations. Again, the the office of presbyter stood in such obvious continuity with that of the elder in the Jewish synagogue that its occupancy by men would seem a foregone conclusion. And yet again, the same may be the case with the office of bishop, though its emergence into prominence is coincidental with the exclusion of the "heresies" in which women held prominent positions to such an extent that it is not possible to proceed without reference to this particular phenomenon.

It is in connection with the "heresies", with the New Prophecy of Montanus as well as with Marcionism and the many gnostic sects, that much of the opposition to the functioning of women first appears. But it is hard to know what to make of the opposition. Much of the writing of the time, from the catholic side, had to do simply with the refutation of the claims of the "heresies" to represent the Gospel. Yet where the functioning of women in the "heresies" is concerned, it tends most frequently to take the form of reference to their brashness or weakness rather than to the relation of their functioning to the theological issues at stake. Indeed, except for the women prophets of Montanism, we are left with considerable uncertainty as to precisely what was the role of women in the "heresies", and whether and in what ways it reflected earlier practices or novel departures.[9] It is a fair guess that the controversies of the second century reinforced the inherited social customs of the catholic communities. But beyond such a guess it is very hard to go.

At a later stage, these customs are further reinforced by new circumstances. The bishops of the period after the persecutions accepted a status equivalent to that of civil magistrates. This new status would have reinforced the exclusion of women, for example. Thus the backlog of custom, supported by scriptural interpretations, led to positive assertions that women were excluded from the episcopacy, many of whose functions were now exercised by the presbyters as well. And a growing awe surrounding the eucharistic species may well have been in part responsible for the attacks in this period on the custom of women's administering the communion, though even here the continuation of the custom among Nestorian and Monophysite Christians may have the same kind of unacknowledged influence as the fear of the "heresies" did earlier.

The outcome of any review of this evidence must be unsatisfactory to all sides in the current issue. Women are practically, if not on principle, excluded from the offices of presbyter and bishop. But the arguments, such as they are, are repetitions of those having to do with continuance of the fallen life rather than with the implications of redemption. On the other hand, we are still — as we must shortly make clear in some detail — very far from a time when the president of the eucharistic assembly was regarded as an *alter christus,* standing in some fashion in the place of Christ, rather than as the offerer of the prayer of the community. Social customs, combined with the convolutions of theological debates and their non-theological impact on the life of the church are the most obvious determiners of the practices of the time. Plain answers to questions which we might like to ask, from whatever position we take with respect to the issues of our time, simply do not come.

When we have come this far, however, we are still in the position of asking the evidence *our own* questions without fully appreciating what the evidence has to say to us — and this is probably truer of the evidence regarding the place of women in this aspect of the life of the church than in any other.

In fact, it is hard for us not to approach early Christian references to deacons, presbtyers, and bishops with the assumption that they are references to a clergy as distinct from laity — a "ministry" as distinct, presumably, from a non-ministry — of the sort with which we have become familiar through our medieval and reformation heritage. But what the evidence actually tells us — what even our much overworked *orans,* which may well picture a veiled virgin, or a bishop, or simply a Christian man or woman held in high esteem tells us — is that there simply was no such thing as a clergy or a "ministry" of the sort that we know. Certainly by the end of our period these persons had become figures of civil as well as religious prominence. As certainly, they were all along regarded as exercising important functions in the life of the community. Yet they still did not constitute a special hierarchy. The fact that the episcopacy was most frequently, though not always, occupied by people who had been presbyters or deacons is chiefly a tribute to their visibility and popularity.[10] Nor were they yet regarded as having any real identity as Christians other than that which they shared with other baptised members of the eucharistic assembly.

It may well seem that we are merely laboring an obvious point, since we are now quite accustomed to talk about the primary importance of one's calling as a member of the church. But inherited notions about a clergy or a ministry are difficult to avoid, as witness the curiously back-handed way in which we now speak of a "ministry of the laity". It is hard for us to grasp what the early Christian evidence has to tell us of a church highly articulated with respect to the various functions of its members and yet clear that these functions are exercised by people whose fundamental status is that of members of the church. What we have is evidence of a period in which there is nothing but a number of "ministries of the laity", the *laos* or people of God. It is a question of perspectives once again. But it may be one which helps us understand why the functioning of women in a "ministry" of the sort with which we are familiar was not likely to arise as a general issue in this period.

Women and "Priesthood" in the church in early Christianity

We must, finally, address the question of whether women did not occupy the offices of bishop and presbyter in the early church because these offices were thought to be means by which a "priesthood of Christ" was exercised in some special way which would have made it impossible for women to occupy them. This is a frequent assumption in current debate both on the part of those who think the practice right and those who think it wrong. Our position is that the early Christian evidence simply does not contain the sort of notion of a "priesthood of Christ" which would make it possible for the subject to arise.

The earliest Christian writings preserved in the New Testament speak of Christ as priest and the church as a priestly body. Nevertheless, neither the title priest nor priestly imagery of any kind is used to describe the work of any particular official in the church. Moreover it is worth noting that there are far fewer references to the church as a priestly body than this generalization would suggest.[11] The real difficulty with this way of putting the matter, however, is that it does not necessarily make clear what the use of priestly and sacrificial imagery is really all about.

It is better to begin by saying that the earliest Christian use of terminology drawn from the Jewish sacrificial *cultus* and its functionaries is "typological" in character, and belongs to the effort to find in the Jewish scriptures foreshadowings of the final action of God now beginning to be manifest in the work of Christ. Looked at in this way, the scriptures could be seen to contain various materials — the Servant figure, the atonement motif, and the sacrificial imagery itself — which foreshadow the self-giving of Christ as fulfilling and transcending the Jewish *cultus* and as opening the way for those in Christ to offer thanksgiving, service, and their own lives to God in concert with him. The result of this approach is the application to Christ and the church of a variety of scriptural references far more extensive than any narrow study of the use of the terms priest and priesthood (*hiereus, hierosune*) would suggest.[12] It is not surprising, however, that there is no notion here of a "priesthood of Christ" exercised by anyone but himself, as the one in association with whom it is possible for Christians to offer themelves to God.

This same "typological" approach governs the elaborations of the priestly and sacrificial imagery which appear in the evidence of the following centuries, and which do include eucharistic references to those who preside at the eucharistic meetings of the church. As liturgical scholars are well aware, these meetings at which bread and wine are offered and partaken are regarded, among other things, as occasions on which the church offers the bloodless sacrifice of the final inbreaking age and holds communion with the coming Christ. Thus Justin Martyr can describe the work of Christ as involving, among other things, teaching us how to offer sacrifices to God; and Irenaeus can enlarge on this point by observing that it is through material things, bread and wine, that we have communion with Christ. It is even conceivable that Justin and Irenaeus could have referred to the "president" of the eucharistic assembly (by Irenaeus' time normally the bishop) , in priestly terms. However, it is first of all in Hippolytus' model prayers for the consecration of a bishop and its attendant eucharistic offering that such terminology appears.

It is also conceivable that the bishop could be referred to as a priest, though to my knowledge — leaving aside the peculiar use of the term in Clement of Rome — it is only Cyprian who seems easily to refer to the episcopal figure as "bishop and priest". But it is a fair guess that disinclination to follow Jewish or pagan precedents, and in the case of the Alexandrians, Clement and Origen, a highly spiritualized view of the Christian life combined with an exceptionally critical attitude toward the Jewish sacrificial *cultus,* account for the omission of the term. However this may be, such a case of the term would imply no more than that the one who offered the bread and wine in the name and presence of the congregation did precisely that. Aside from the curiously and richly complicated imagery by which Christ's offering and that of those in Christ are interrelated, there is no way in which a "priesthood of Christ" different from that of the whole church would make any sense at all.

It is when we come to the Constantinian Peace of the Church that it becomes fairly common — though certainly not universal — for the bishop and those associated in his work to be referred to as priests, and their function as that of priesthood. Reasons for this development seem fairly obvious. Despite continued rejection of the notion that Christianity contained any precise equivalent of the Levitical priesthood, there was no reason not to employ priestly terminology to describe the functions of those who offered sacrifices to God. Anyone familiar with the situation of the church in this period, its new willingness to adopt terminology heretofore suspect, will find it easy to understand the increasing use of this terminology. It is, in any case, in this period that we encounter the great works on the responsibilities of the Christian leadership, the works of Gregory of Nazianzus and John Chrysostom, of Ambrose and Gregory the Great. One might presumably turn to these works to discover what significance this period attaches to the use of the terms priest and priesthood.

It is just here, however, in the period immediately prior to that in which later views of the Christian priesthood took shape and in works assiduously read by the formulators of those views, that we most clearly discern the fact that early Christian uses of priest and priesthood arise from a perspective very different from those we have inherited. In fact, the writings in question do not seem to us to discuss what we have come to regard as the substantial issue about priest and priesthood. Rather, they deal with the awesome responsibilities which fall on the persons engaged in the work and offer advice as to how it is possible to shoulder them.

The first piece of this literature, Gregory of Nazianzus' oration "On [his] flight" from the responsibilities he finally assumed as associate of his father in that see, does not deal specifically with the functions of the bishop or use priestly terminology, but employs a wealth of illustrations from the history of Israel and the church to show what an impossible thing it is for any one to serve as a teacher, preacher, and pastor of a congregation of diverse people without the development of inner resources virtually beyond imagining.

Chrysostom's "On the priesthood", written while the author was still a presbyter but directed, as the title suggests, to the full range of episcopal functions, begins by referring to the terrifying prospect of being one through whose actions and words Christians are born at Baptism and the Lord's body made present at the Eucharist. But as the work unfolds, it is the line taken by Nazianzus restated with considerable detail regarding the work of the preacher and pastor.

Ambrose' "On the duties of ministers," is actually the work of a bishop, but stands in a curious relation to the rest of this literature. We have other works of his which represent his preaching and catechizing, and unfold his views of Baptism and Eucharist. This work is, except for an initial reference to his extraordinary election to the "priesthood", an attempt to draw on Cicero's "On the duties" of public officials for counsel in the virtues required of Christian leaders.

Finally, Gregory the Great's "Pastoral Rule", stands more in the line of Nazianzen and Chrysostom, and is an effort to make their considerations available for Latin readers as part of the famous pope's interest in instilling a sense of responsibility in the Italian episcopate in the difficult time in which he occupied the Roman see. The interest of all of these works lies more in the style of piety or view of the Christian life in general which they bring to bear on the work of the bishop rather than on any precise relationship between sacramental theology and views of the priesthood — the relationship which now seems so natural to us.

This is not to say that these works lack interest. They are extremely interesting for anyone who reads them from their own perspective. They reveal the pressing need for those who were bishops — or, as in the case of Nazianzen and Chrysostom when they wrote, associates of bishops who already had an important share of their work — for help in dealing with the problems of functioning in the new circumstances which the popularity of the Christian movement and the confusions of the times had forced upon them. They attempt to fill this need by applying the insights of Christian spirituality, the techniques of rhetoric, and a great deal of common sense to these problems. In the case of Chrysostom in particular, it is possible to discern the great aura of mystery which now surrounds the baptismal and eucharistic rites, and which at least for him makes the office of bishop even more awesome to contemplate.

The difficulty with these works, from our perspective, is that they do not address the subject of "priesthood" in the way we assume it should be addressed, and certainly not in the way they were made to address it when many of their references to the inner life and external responsibilities of the bishops were applied to those who were thought to stand in the place of Christ in the dramatic sacrifice of the mass as it came to be viewed in the medieval period. They do not contain a view of the bishops and their associates as exercising a special "priesthood of Christ" which virtually make the eucharistic celebrant an *alter Christus*. Insofar as they treat, directly or by allusion, the liturgical functions of those now described as "priests", they are most easily read as continuing the view of the preceding centuries rather than as anticipating those of the centuries to come. The *alter Christus* theme, frequently mentioned in current debate, comes from a different environment altogether, from a time when it was necessary to interpret the visual motions of the celebrant as an allegory of the life of Christ and when it was common to take the saying of mass to be part of the celebrant's personal growth in the life of Christ.[13]

We began this section on the question of whether women were excluded from the office of bishop and presbyter because these offices were thought to be the means by which the "priesthood of Christ" was exercised in a way which virtually excluded them from consideration. What we have tried to suggest is that the use of priestly and sacrificial imagery in the early Christian evidence is such that there is no place for a "priesthood of Christ" of the sort assumed by the question. Indeed, by the time that the great works just mentioned were written, the occupancy by men of the offices in question was already a matter which had been decided by inherited tradition and social convention rather than on theological grounds.

To put the matter in this way will please neither those who want the early Christian evidence to speak against the inclusion of women in the office of bishop or presbyter nor those who want it to speak in its favor. To my mind, the evidence shows clearly that priestly and sacrificial imagery could and was used of the life of the church in ways which apply equally to women and men. Even so, that imagery is not used in a way which allows it to be applied directly to the current issues. And we must, after all, deal with the evidence in its own right. The truth of the matter would seem to be that, once again, it must be looked at from a perspective very different from our own.

Some reflections

It might seem that it has been our purpose to render the evidence of early Christianity irrelevant to the issues of the present. It is truer to say that it has been part of our purpose to suggest that too great an involvement with the issues of the present can make this evidence unintelligible and hence irrelevant to us.

But what is its relevance? We do not live in the early Christian era, face its problems, or attempt to deal with them with its assumptions and insights. We live in our own time, face our own problems, and have to deal with them with our own assumptions and insights. It has been a recurrent danger in western Christianity to expect help of the wrong sort from the past, and then either to be critical of the past or to force it to be different from what it was. On the whole the critics are the more impressive, since they at least grasp that there is some problem involved. But they are not necessarily any more correct.

In the present instance, it seems to me that the early Christian conviction that the distinction of "male and female" was abrogated in Christ looms much larger when set within the context of that time than we are likely to appreciate when we look at the evidence from our point of view. The way in which this conviction was reflected in the life of the church, in its liturgical meetings, in its celebration of women martyrs and ascetics, and so forth, was of much greater significance than we are likely to realize. Certainly assumptions and conventions inherited from both paganism and Judaism are evident in the way in which the life of the church was constructed. But we ought to be able to take them for what they were — assumptions and conventions of that time rather than ours. In particular, this seems to me the case with the functioning of women in what we now call the "ministry" of the church. The appearance of women as deacons but not as presbyters or bishops is certainly largely a reflection of the circumtances of the time. Efforts to make it more than this are inconclusive as efforts to discover serious reasons for the exclusion of women from certain of the offices. It is now commonly said that there are no "theological objections" to the functioning of women as presbyters and bishops, and I should judge that the early Christian evidence — if left to speak for itself — can be cited in support of this dictum.

But to me there is a far larger issue for us to ponder. The

principal claim of the early church was to be a manifestation of the inbreaking power of God in the midst of the powers governing the life of the world. What was said and done about the abrogation of the distinction of "male and female" in Christ was said in relation to this claim. This claim naturally made little sense during the time when the church's attention was directed toward the building of a Christian society in the aftermath of the collapse of the Roman *imperium*. It is beginning to make a good deal more sense in our time, in which the vestigial remains of Christendom — including the distinction of clergy and laity — survive in yet another, and far more confusing set of circumstances.

To ponder what it might mean in our own time to be church in the early Christian sense, is the first priority for modern Christians. Indeed, concern with the place of women in the church is most evident where this problem is being pondered. One result of such pondering may well be, as I think it will, the admission of women to the orders of presbyter and bishop, since the conventions of our time no longer impede it. But other results of such pondering may well be far more surprising than that.

<hr />

NOTES

1 It is easy to see the *orans* in question through the reproductions, in color in G. Gassiot-Talabot, ROMAN AND PALAEO-CHRISTIAN PAINTING (New York: Funk and Wagnalls, 1965), p. 74 (commentary p. 187), and in black and white in W. Lowrie, ART IN THE EARLY CHURCH (New York: Harper Torchbooks, 1965), plate 16. Neither reproduction makes clear that the white portions surrounding the head are the results of damage to the wall.

2 The *orantes* have been interpreted in many ways. We take Lowrie's view (ART IN THE EARLY CHURCH, pp. 45ff.) that those which represent Christians buried at the particular sites show them alive at prayer. But there is surely more to the matter. The praying position is used in the depiction of figures from Israel's history as well as from the early Church. It is quite clearly a means of identifying those who belong to the people of God which is being assembled in anticipation of the Kingdom.

3 The problem is an instance of "anachronism", that bane of all historians, which is admittedly the easiest charge to bring against those who take a different view from your own. The slow effort to place early Christianity in its contemporary setting has still not done much to overcome the influence of the divergent 19th century views which saw early Christianity either as a departure from the original Gospel as a result of philosophical or institutional concerns, or as in some sense still the touch-stone of Christian life and thought it had long been taken to be.

4 Of the number of works reflecting the recent recovery of the centrality of the

liturgical meetings for all aspects of early Christian life, the comprehensive work of A. Schmemann, *Introduction to Liturgical Theology* (London: Faith, 1966) should be noted. In many places (e.g. pp. 60ff., 78ff.) it touches on the importance of the liturgical meetings as defining the nature of the Church as a manifestation of the eschatological people of God in the sense assumed in these remarks.

5 For the *passio* of Perpetua see volume 3 of the ANTE-NICENE FATHERS, pp. 697 ff. Ptolemy's letter to Flora can be found in J. Stevenson's NEW EUSEBIUS (London: SPCK: 1957), extract 69. See also Jerome's LETTERS, especially 22, and Methodius' *De cibis* 1.1-2, and *De sanguisuga.* For a picture of Macrina and Monica see Gregory's *De anima et resurrectione* or Augustine's *De beata vita.*

6 H. van der Meer, WOMEN PRIESTS IN THE CATHOLIC CHURCH (Philadelphia: Temple University Press, 1973) offers the most readily available collection of references, though the focus of the work is the priesthood.

7 For an introduction to the close relation of martyrdom and asceticism and their appeal to the contemporary world, see W. H. C. Frend: MARTYRDOM AND PERSECUTION IN THE EARLY CHURCH (Dover: 1967) and E. R. Dodds: PAGAN AND CHRISTIAN IN AN AGE OF ANXIETY (Cambridge University Press, 1965).

8 Irenaeus, ADVERSUS HAERESES 3.1ff.

9 Cf. H. van der Meer (see note 6) for a comprehensive catalogue of the evidence. Women clearly functioned not merely as Montanist prophets but in various capacities in Marcionite and Gnostic communities, and it seems clear that it was in reaction to this that the arguments supposed to show the subordinate place of women in the life of the Church were given prominence.

10 It is true that the canons of the synod of Serdica A.D. 342 suggest that those in important positions should be elected from those who have proved themselves in less important ones, and that these canons can seem, on a later reading, to suggest a hierarchy of offices. In fact it is the intention of these canons to secure a local ministry free from external pressures of the sort common at the time. In any case, they were not commonly adhered to, and were treated, as were other early Christian canons, as sage advice rather than as legislation. At a later time, however, they did provide precedent for the elaboration of a much more structured hierarchy of orders than they themselves envisage.

11 The most familiar reference to the Church as a priestly body is in I Pt 2:5. Another is in 5:10. See also Jn 17:17 - 19. The Pauline *corpus* speaks of the sacrifice of Christians in Rom 12:11 and Phil 4:18, though of course the whole motif of baptismal death and resurrection (Rom 6.3ff., Gal 3.27ff.) is replete with sacrificial features. It is, of course, important to sort these references out into strands of interpretation, as well as to take account of the related references of a "priestly" character. It remains true, however, that there are fewer references to the priestly character of the Church than later generalizations would suggest.

12 To illustrate our point, by and large the Synoptic materials conflate the Servant and the atonement themes, as in Mk 10:33ff., esp. 45; Mt 16:21, 20:28 (leaving aside the special emphasis of Lk 18:31 on the death of the prophets as foreshadowing that of Christ). The same conflation is already present in the Pauline stress on Christ's death for others, as in Rom 5:10ff., Eph 5:2,

cf. 1 Cor 11:26. The Johannine theme is that of Christ's making himself holy, as in the famous Jn 17:1ff., esp. 17:19. See also Ap 5:6ff. The most extended use of priestly and sacrificial imagery, of course, is that in Heb 2:17ff., 4:14ff., 5:20ff., 8:1ff., 9:11ff., in which Christ's self-offering is interpreted as a fulfillment of the promise contained in the figure of Melchizedek. However, a very great number of references having to do with offering, thanksgiving, righteousness, and death take on priestly and sacrificial overtones in the contexts in which they occur.

13 See J. Jungmann, MASS OF THE ROMAN RITE (New York: Benziger, 1951), vol. 1, pp. 233ff., and more generally T. Klauser, A SHORT HISTORY OF THE WESTERN LITURGY (London: Oxford University Press, 1969), esp. pp. 49ff., 109ff. It is not hard to see how this different environment would allow the writings of the earlier period to be read in a very different fashion from that intended.

4 Christ, Revelation, and the Ordination of Women

Arthur A. Vogel

Because Christian ministry in its very essence is a sending by Christ, no person — male or female — exercises a right in respect to it. No one has a right to ordination, and no one can demand ordination. Vocation, from the first calling of the disciples by Christ, has been seen as a call from God, not an impetus from human beings. Even when a person has felt called by God, the church has judged (as best it could) whether or not the call be genuine. It would be a perversion of its nature and a betrayal of its mission if the church were pressured by outside forces to act contrary to its mind in such a matter. Christ, not the social factions of the day, is the head of the body. That having been said, the question presently facing the church is, what kind of considerations *prior* to those of a given person preclude ordination? Does, for example, being female preclude it?

— I —

Let us look first at some of the arguments which are used against ordaining women to the presbyterate and episcopate.

1. Throughout the Judeo-Christian tradition God the Creator has been referred to as the Father. Does not the Fatherhood of God give a uniqueness to a male typology and symbolization of God? As such, only males should be commissioned by ordination in the Father's name for the roles assigned to

presbyters and bishops in the liturgical and hierarchical life of the church.

2. In the Incarnation, the Word took flesh as a male; thus only a male can sacramentally share in and represent the priesthood of Christ.

3. Christ chose only men to be apostles.

4. The church is the bride of Christ, and presbyters and bishops represent Christ to the church; women cannot represent the bridegroom.

5. Equality between the sexes is not the same thing as identity of the sexes; "equality" does not mean "to do the same thing." The ordination of women within the church involves different issues than those addressed by the women's liberation movement in the secular community.

6. Because of the respect for tradition in the Roman Catholic Orthodox, and Anglican Churches, none of the aforementioned Churches should unilaterally move to ordain women as priests or bishops. Contemporary ecumenical consensus is necessary for such a radical departure from tradition. Moreover, there would be serious ecumenical consequences for any Anglican Church with the Roman Catholic and Orthodox Churches if an Anglican Church unilaterally ordained women to an order of ministry other than the diaconate.

Prior to presenting the positive argument which convinces me that women should be able to be ordained to all orders of ministry, I will respond briefly to the just-listed contrary arguments which are already in the field.

First of all, the Fatherhood of God does not seem to be an adequate basis upon which to exclude women from ordination to the priesthood because "Fatherhood," when applied to God, itself transcends masculinity: God transcends sex in it entirety. The key to the issue in this regard seems to be whether the ordained priesthood should primarily testify to God the Father's transcendence of everything created (including sex) and to God the Son's transcendence of the Old Testament priesthood, or primarily testify to the descriptive, historical mode of God's presence in the man Jesus Christ.

That God's immanence in the world depends upon his transcendence — that God's presence with us depends upon his difference from us — seems to give the primacy to God's transcendence. God's difference from us is always the first thing which must be stressed about him: only so can we begin to comprehend his love in coming to us.

Concerning the second argument that the Word took flesh as male, it has well been pointed out by Dr. E. L. Mascall that it was "male human nature" not a male human person in which the Word became flesh. Jesus was not a good man adopted by God. On the other hand, Jesus was conceived in the womb of a "female human person." If the Gospel story of the virgin birth is accepted as historically descriptive of the birth — instead of being only a device for stating the religious truth that God is Jesus' Father — then Jesus' birth as a male takes on special significance. In a parthenogenic birth the child would have to be a female; if a son were born to a virgin by divine initiative, the genetic change involved would indicate a special purpose of God.

Granting all that has just been said, however, God the Father might have explicitly chosen (and achieved by a virgin birth) to enflesh the Word in male humanity for reasons we would think of today as "social" rather than "theological." The fact that only male witnesses were juridically acceptable at the time, and the fact that Jesus came to bear witness to the Father, would be sufficient grounds for the Father's choice. But we must admit that such a reason might not have been sufficient ground for that choice either. The inconclusiveness of our arguments should be acknowledged. The point is, the actual choice of the Father of male human nature does not *necessitate* one theoretical explanation by human beings as over against another. Once more, the transcendence of God's Fatherhood precludes our assuming too much for any human typological interpretation of his acts.

Moreover, even though the Word became flesh in the man Jesus, the human condition redeemed in Jesus contains within it the masculine and feminine polarities. There is no doubt that these two polarities are found within the redeemed community, the mystical body of Christ, and within the general, royal priesthood of the church.

It is argued by some that sexual difference prevents a woman from representing Christ's priesthood and from participating in that priesthood in the ordained, representative order. This contention can be sustained, however, only if it can be further shown that there is a sense in which Christ's priesthood is restricted to masculinity. Here the transcendence of God and his revelation to human beings in Christ again enters the picture. As Christ's priesthood fulfills, surpasses, and terminates the Old Testament priesthood, the exclusion of women from the latter does not seem, in itself, to exclude women from the former. The transcendence of, and difference of Christ's priesthood from, the Old Testament model might well be shown by the inclusion of women — someone different — in it.

The argument against ordaining women to presbyteral and episcopal ministries I think the strongest is the one noting that Christ chose only men to be his apostles. The argument is strong because its basis is descriptive rather than theoretical; it begins with a premise that everyone must accept. To depart from Christ's action in this regard is to change the *descriptive* norm of the Bible. The Bible has been and remains a source of immediate comfort to people because it is not a theoretical text arguing to certain debatable conclusions. It is a book of testimony and witness about something which is claimed actually to have happened; the historical description of life and death which it contains is something with which we can immediately identify in our own lives. An argument based on Christ's actual choices, therefore, is an argument based on the Bible's highest level of Christian conviction: it is based on a description of what actually happened.

One cannot argue against Christ's actual choices, for Christ has already made them. Granting the descriptive fact, however, one may still ask whether or not the action described in time past was meant to be a norm for all future time. We should again recall that only men could serve as witnesses in court in our Lord's time and culture, and the apostles were sent to be witnesses. An analogy is sometimes offered between Christ's attitude about slavery and the fact that he chose no women to be his apostles. The contention runs that as our Lord accepted slavery — and we no longer accept his lead there — so, although he chose only men to be his apostles, we need not follow his lead there either.

The analogy is not a good one, however, because too many extraneous elements can influence it. Too much depends upon a presumed knowledge of the intimate mind of Christ. Christ's attitude toward slavery refers to an effect of his proclamation on society; besides, there is good reason to believe that Christ himself expected the parousia soon to occur. The choice of his apostles, on the other hand, involves Christ's own "initiative of revelation" — not its effect on society.

For the reasons suggested above, I believe no interpretative argument for the ordination of women will ever have the immediate conviction of a description of the acts of Christ himself. That does not deny the possible truth of an interpretative argument about his acts, but it does state a fact proponents of the ordination of women should recognize.

The argument that the church is the bride of Christ and that women cannot represent the bridegroom has an immediate appeal and consistency. The argument is attenuated, however, when we go on to consider that the existence of holy orders is coterminal with the existence of the church in this world. Orders are sacraments, and sacraments are sacraments of the church. All orders of clergy stand within the church and so all orders necessarily partake of the nature of the bride, even when men are ordained to the orders.

I most heartily concur with the fifth contention that "equality" does not mean "identity." In the order of redemption women are in no way inferior to men, and differences between men and women must not be ranked on a scale of superiority and inferiority. The oft quoted text from Galatians 3:38 in which there is said to be no such thing as male and female in Christ contextually refers to initiation into Christ, in contrast to the initiatory rite of circumcision in the Old Testament. To try to argue from this text to the ordination of women is, in my opinion, to extrapolate beyond the intention of the text.

A difficulty permeating all discussion of the equality through difference of the sexes is present-day confusion about the nature of sexuality itself. Some people and schools of thought are clear about the matter, but there is little consensus among the totality of people and schools. Conflicting and competing views on the nature of sex are a complicating factor in the issue facing the church which the church will not be able to resolve by its own decision — whatever that decision is. Data will come from beyond its competence.

Finally, concern for tradition in the life of the Anglican Communion along with the Roman Catholic and Orthodox

Churches, is an undeniable fact and should not be taken lightly. Tradition is a community's lived fidelity to itself; Christian tradition must be fidelity to Christ. But the merit attaching to respect for tradition is based upon respect for the truth which tradition preserves. In the final analysis, it must be truth — tradition insofar as it is true — which the church follows in the name of Christ, not just custom. If the church (or a church) is convinced that something is true, departure from custom to embrace the truth must be construed as life in the Spirit of tradition. The departure would be from *a* tradition, not *the* tradition.

A truly ecumenical council of the church is desirable at any time about any major issue in the life of the church. But the realities of the church and the world being what they presently are — that is to say, the sin of human beings recognized for what it is — it is wistful, to say the least, to project an ecumenical council truly representative of Christendom in the near future. To argue that only such a council can determine the immediate choice of a church on the issue at hand is to deny the primacy of conscience in every Christian decision. Each person is called by God to give allegiance to the truth as prudently as he can in the circumstances in which he lives. Where general councils cannot be called, decisions must be made beneath that conciliar level, although they should always be made on the broadest consensus possible. The ecumenical consequences of an act by a church must be seriously taken into account in any prudent deliberation about the act, but, once again, truth — not the consequences of choosing the truth — must be the ultimate criterion in decision making.

— II —

Turning now to the positive argument I suggest for the ordination of women to the presbtyerate and episcopacy, we are led to consider the mystery of God's most intimate life as we know that life in the revelation of Jesus Christ and the Spirit.

Many arguments against ordaining women to the presbyteral and episcopal orders are based on the Fatherhood of God. The Fatherhood of God is a "given" in the Christian revelation and cannot be compromised. The Fatherhood of God encompasses the relationship of every creature to God, but, in the fullness of Christian revelation — in the intimate life of God revealed to us — the Father is but one Person of the Trinity.

In traditional trinitarian theology a type of priority is claimed for the Father over the Son and Holy Spirit. But nowhere are creaturely categories more inadequate than in trying to describe God's life. Thus, as soon as the priority of the Father is stated, it is given severe qualification. For example, the priority is said to be neither temporal nor essential: the Father did not exist *before* the Son and Holy Spirit, nor is the Father more God than the other Persons of the Trinity.

"Properly understood" no Person of the Trinity can be known apart from the other Persons: the Persons indwell each other, and the Persons can ultimately be described only by their relations to each other, not by derivation from a norm such as human sexuality. The uniqueness of the Christian understanding of God consists in the contention that the one God is, in some mysterious way, a loving, knowing community of Persons. The fullness of Person, even in God, is thus seen to be person in community. "Person" and "community" are not external realities: persons can be their full selves only in community, and true community is always a community of persons.

If the mysterious community of Persons in the Godhead were taken, as I think it should, as the primary Christian revelation of God's nature, human persons in community would be seen to be better analogical symbolization of God than the sex of human beings taken individually.

Community depends upon difference. That truth is necessary to understand many of the ancient trinitarian controversies. The ultimate mind of the patristic church was, for example, that each Person of the Trinity is a complete and unique Person in himself: God is not just one Person who appears in different modes or masks. Thus a Greek word (*hypostasis*), which normally referred to concrete individuals became applied to each of the Persons of the Trinity in orthodox usage to show each Person's distinctness from the other Persons. The terminology adopted — applying, as it did, to material entities in the world — was the most scandalous that could be used about a nonmaterial God. Use of the term proclaimed the distinctness and difference of the Persons of the Trinity from each other in a way which could never be compromised. Community is founded upon difference even in the Godhead, and the difference of the trinitarian Persons from each other cannot be diluted.

In the human order, sex is one type of difference among

persons and so is constitutive of human community. There can be human community among persons of the same sex, but the Judeo-Chritian tradition has always seen sex in its communal role. In the creation story as told in the second chapter of Genesis (v. 18), God created woman because "it is not good that man should be alone." Woman was therefore created to constitute the fullness of human community. The first chapter of Genesis (v. 27) indicates that the "image of God" extends to both male and female.

All of these factors taken into consideration, a convincing case can be made that the communal, trinitarian nature of God would better be shown by a presbyteral community embodying the fullness of human difference in community, as God created that difference, than could be shown by an all-male community alone.

This is the place to make one or two more remarks about the Fatherhood of God. We have already noted that God transcends sex, so the "Fatherhood" of God does not mean God is male. We have also noted that mother love and father love are constitutive of human relations and that, after the example of Christ himself, Christians are told to call God *Abba*. Because God as *Abba*, Father, transcends human sexuality we should not be surprised to find that attempts to explicate God's Fatherhood in terms of male typology alone prove woefully inadequate. God, as source of mother love, contains and manifests that love eminently within his Fatherhood. Julian of Norwich, a fifteenth century English anchoress, never wished to compromise the Fatherhod of God or maleness of Christ; yet she spoke of the "Motherhood" of God and even called Christ "Mother Jesus," when she compared him feeding us with himself in the Eucharist to a mother's feeding of her child.

As described by Erich Fromm, mother love founds us in being, making us secure and glad to be alive. Mother love is unconditional, the love of acceptance and nurture. That very love of acceptance, mercy, and nurture — characteristics of mother love — is intrinsic to the understanding of God as "Father" in Joachim Jeremias' chapter "Abba," in THE CENTRAL MESSAGE OF THE NEW TESTAMENT. Jesus Christ, our acceptance by and nurture from the Father, reveals that the Father cannot be understood in terms of abstract, male typology alone. Such a revelation by a *Son* is testimony that he is, indeed, the transcendent Word of a unique and transcendent Father. Through our acceptance and unconditional love by the Father through the Son we know it is good simply to be alive. That is the feeling infants should first receive from their mothers.

Turning from remarks about "fatherhood," we may well turn our attention toward "priesthood." Let us look at the New Testament doctrine. There can be no doubt that in the New Testament Jesus Christ is the one and only great High Priest. His priesthood is unique, taken from no human being. It is also a well-known fact that nowhere in the New Testament are ministers called priests. In 1 Peter 2:9 Christians are said to be "a chosen race, a royal priesthood, a holy nation," in a manner referring directly to Exodus 19:6, "and you shall be to me a kingdom of priests and a holy nation." The priesthood of Exodus 19, it is pointed out, applies to Israel as a collective whole (the reference is not to a priesthood distributed to individuals); it is not a priesthood of the Levitical type. The latter is a particular priesthood instituted for ritual, cultic purposes. The royal priesthood of Israel involves the community as a whole and is primarily concerned with Israel's witness to God before the nations of the world.

The suggestion is made that Christians should not confuse the particular, ritualistic priesthood (based on the Levitical model) with the royal priesthood of the whole People of God (based on the Exodus model). Viewed in that perspective, the particular, ordained priesthood is not a "specification" and "intensification" of the royal priesthood every Christian enters by baptism. Thus it would be wrong to argue that, since men and women are already found within the royal priesthood, no new theological issue is involved in admitting women to the particular priesthood. But whatever view a person takes of the relation of the particular priesthood to the royal priesthood, one point is clear: the particular priesthood exists for the enablement of the universal, royal priesthood. Witness in the world to the all-sufficiency of Christ's High Priesthood is the purpose of the universal priesthood of the church. The particular priesthood exists for, and is in the service of, the universal priesthood.

The ordained ministry is called into being *for* the royal priesthood — for the community — to enable it to be itself and to make its witness in the world. In a basic way, the needs of the royal priesthood are determinative of the particular priesthood.

In its witness to the Fatherhood of God, the witness of the royal priesthood to the world is a ministry of reconciliation. That being the case, specialized Christian ministries, including the particular priesthood, must themselves be enabling agencies of reconciliation. The purpose of all Christian ministry is to build, not destroy, godly community.

To ordain women to the presbyteral and episcopal orders is, I believe, to take something of a chance, but I also believe the chance is worth taking if it is done by community for community.

5 Women, the Priesthood and Catholicism

Urban T. Holmes

The mainstream of the Christian tradition over the last two thousand years lies within one cultural pattern, the Graeco-Roman world, with two basic variations upon the fundamental theme, the Eastern and the Western. Certainly there have been and are exceptions to this. There is, for example, the ancient Mar Thoma Church of India, the indigenous remnants of sixteenth century Jesuit missionary activity in the Far East, and some nativistic Christian groups in Africa. These elements have not been, however, in any sense a part of the cultural context which has been the shaping influence upon the understanding of the religious experience which we call Christian theology.

In fact, the intellectual world in which the Christian tradition has evolved is so monochrome that undoubtedly many are incapable of identifying the process by which the transcendent experience of God necessarily takes on the texture, color, and form of a given culture. Perhaps we are aware of the anomaly of building eleventh century English Romanesque churches in Kenya, Fiji or western Kansas on the grounds that this is "what a church is supposed to look like," but are we equally aware that a patriarchal society, characteristic of the heirs of Greek and Roman thought, produces a masculine notion of God, which when imposed upon a matriarchal society might be just as much an anomaly? We speak of the "faith once delivered to the saints" and the "mind of the Church," often without realizing that we are identifying the divine intentionality with cultural patterns of a relatively short span of human history within a limited social context.

It would be gratuitous in the extreme to suggest that we despise our Graeco-Roman culture, Western or Eastern. Whether or not it has come to the end of its productivity, as some say, is debatable; but we are our culture, and we can no more deny it than we can deny our natural parents. We do need to understand, however, that language, norms of human inter-action, symbols and myths, aesthetic values, etc. are elements of culture. While our culture provides us with the only available tools of theological thought, and we ought to be thankful for them, they inevitably produce a distorted representation of any experience they describe. This is true no matter how reasoned a use we make of these tools, since our community necessarily influences our use of reason itself.[1] Therefore, while we are grateful for the richness of a cultural heritage such as the mainstream of Christianity has possessed in the profundity of the Greek and Roman mind, nonetheless we must use its gift with humility. We need to be careful not to claim an *absolute* quality for what only the ineffable mind of God can possess.

This issue comes into sharp focus on the matter of the ordination of women to the priesthood. There have been those who have said that there are *no* theological reasons why women should *not* be ordained priest. There have even been those who have claimed that it is a matter of theological indifference. Both of these observations represent a negative theological approach to the question. Actually the debate over the ordination of women to the priesthood raises at least one very important theological issue and makes a positive contribution at no less than two levels to the whole theological process. The one very important issue is that of the elusive problem of speaking of God in a given cultural context. The two levels at which it contributes to the task of theology are, first, as a challenge to the masculine theology of the patriarchal Graeco-Roman culture of which we are a part; and, second, as a possible stimulus for a more catholic expression of the experience of God.

The reason why the question of the ordination of women to the priesthood lies in the area of a positive theology is related to the function of the priest. Quite aside from the doctrine of the priesthood, the person of the priest is a very powerful force in representing completely the experience of God. Speaking practically, the priest has a focal role in those events — liturgy, teaching, preaching, counseling — in which we consciously seek the mediation of God to humanity. It does not matter whether we are speaking of the preacher in the Puritan meeting house or the celebrant at a Solemn High Mass. The person of the priest takes on a symbolic function, irrespective of our theology of the church, the sacraments, or the ministry. He is a pivotal figure.

In the First Letter to the Corinthians Paul complains of division in the church, "When one says, 'I am Paul's man,' and another, 'I am for Apollos.'" He adds, "Are you not all too human? After all, what is Apollos? What is Paul? We are simply God's agents in bringing you to faith" (1 Cor 3:4 - 5). Paul is being naive, perhaps intentionally. The agent which Apollos and Paul and every priest is becomes identified with that God for which he is the agent.

Every clergyman has the frequent experience of being called "God" by little children. The child differs from the adult only in that the process of equating the one represented with the one representing is transparent. This is why I speak of the priest as the "sacramental person."[2] It is something of what Luther meant when he said that a person is *larva Dei*, "the mask of God."[3] No one has seen God, but we have seen the one who stands in for God; and while this can be and is any person since we are all made in God's image, this function is focused in that person authorized to preside at the Eucharist, preach, and bless and absolve in God's name — that is, to do the godly actions.

This is a difficult point for some because, as I suspect, the priest was for centuries a civic official and has recently become a professional, and neither model adequately conveys the symbolic function of the priest.[4] Both fail to capture the fact that to be a priest means to live for that which transcends the commonwealth and is above human knowledge and skills, as well as to be a means of participation in the transcendent One. Surely this makes a large claim for a human agent! Henri Nouwen's image of the priest as the "wounded healer," however, who restores wholeness by making his own brokenness and search for healing available to others enables us to see that such an understanding of the clergyman is not one of presumption, but of surrender to the love of God.[5]

The person of the priest, his very being, becomes then part of the substance of our almost instinctive image of God, and the stuff from which theology is made. Perhaps this is not true of one priest or a half dozen, but it is true of the composite of priesthood as consistently reinforced in so many times and places. The priest is symbol and, as Paul Ricoeur has said, "symbol invites thought" (or invites to do theology) .[6] The masculine priesthood evokes a masculine image of God, and the masculine image of God makes a male priesthood part of the will of God.

Much of the women's liberation movement has broken into this circle by pointing out that the attributes of gender are a product of culture and that the person is not its sexuality. It must be carefully noted that this is going beyond the earlier suggestion that the exclusively masculine interpretation of God is a product of the patriarchal Graeco-Roman culture. There is nothing absolute, as I have already said, about this excessively masculine emphasis. It might appear then that I agree with their point of view that the denial of ordination to the priesthood to women is merely an ideological question and has nothing to do with theological truth.[7] This is not, however, the case.

Certainly there is a great deal of evidence that the bulk of behavior patterns and attitudes we attribute to gender is culturally induced, even if we do not underestimate the power of culture. For example, while it may be culturally accepted, it is not in accord with "human nature," as far as we can tell, that women cry more than men, that women are more religious than men, that men make better artists than women, or that women like to keep house more than men.

There is a danger, however, that in affirming this truth we miss one that suggests there is more to the question of the ordination of women to the priesthood than the acknowledgement of the relativity of cultural images. If we say, as we have, that Christian theology has been shaped in one cultural pattern and that this has given the tradition a peculiar texture, color, and form, this is *not* to say that there is not a resource for theology that underlies the multiplicity of cultures and has a universal quality. At least some scholars would suggest there is such a universal context. Carl Jung spoke of the collective unconscious; ethologists such as Konrad Lorenz and Desmond Morris describe the genetic patterning of behavior; Noam Chomsky, a linguist, refers to the deep grammar; and anthropologists look for what is common to all mankind, if it only amounts to the incest taboo.[8]

The universality of the dying and rising God, the prevalence of the sacred meal, and the sense that death is not the end of what is valuable in a life are examples of images embedded in the underlying resource, which are available to all cultures. Where some in the women's liberation movement overstate their case is in their failure — as understandable as it may be — to grasp the very likely possibility that the *masculine and feminine symbols,* joined in a creative tension, are also located within that underlying resource. This is to say there is possibly more to gender than culture. To be a person is not to be asexual. There is no such creature! To be a person is to possess, not as part of its cultural heritage, but of its human heritage, that symbolic reality (the most powerful reality of all) of masculinity and femininity in interaction.

Without attempting to describe extensively the nature of the masculine and feminine symbols and their relation to one another, briefly they can be identified with the thought patterns traditionally associated with the right and left hands, respectively, as attributed in Robert Ornstein's research in the functions of the left and right hemispheres of the brain.[9] The masculine is associated with the dextrous, the explicit, the analytical, the causal, the active, the creative, etc. The feminine in turn is related to the sinister, the tacit, the ambiguous, the spontaneous, the receptive, the nonlineal, etc.

The masculine is not the possession of the male individual to the exclusion of the feminine nor is the feminine the possession of the female individual to the exclusion of the masculine. Sometimes women who have followed in general agreement to this point will resist the possibility of a male writing about the feminine, because "he knows nothing about it." This is not true for the male who is seeking to understand himself in his entirety. In fact, for the man who has struggled with the feminine symbol within his own inner resources there may be greater understanding than in the woman who has taken it for granted.

Historically man has denied the feminine symbol within himself to his own peril. This has been true of man particularly when he is a member of a patriarchal society, such as our Graeco-Roman culture. It is evidenced in the male's attempt to protect himself from the feminine symbol within himself as much as from without by forming exclusive male associations.[10] The more we are threatened by the feminine the more frantically the males exclude the females from certain places, times, and activities. The feminine is often seen as "polluting." Just to name some contemporary examples, there is the hunting camp, the club or the bar (depending on one's social class), the secret society, and until recently the corporate structure. The Roman Curia is another example, which the priestly establishment might take to heart. Certainly the reaction of some priests in recent years to the ordination of women to the priesthood has taken on more the characteristics of finding that a woman has joined the fraternity than of commitment to the Gospel of Jesus Christ.

If the masculine and feminine symbols and their interrelation are the common resource of every person, which underlies and extends far beyond their particular cultural conditioning, it has to be also said that the male individual is more likely to bring into consciousness the masculine symbol and the female individual the feminine symbol. In other words, a significant meeting with a woman is going to evoke in a person the possibility of interpreting all that touches upon that experience in terms of the feminine. There is no doubt, for example, that the presence of a woman in a social gathering heightens the awareness and deepens the respect for the portentous implications of obscenity.[11] In the same way when a male is the consistent adept at ritual functions we attribute to the God he invokes notions of law-giving, single-minded clarity, initiative, and mastery.

There is nothing wrong with such notions of God, *as far as they go*. The problem is that in an excessively masculine society, whose patriarchal culture has consistently sought to repress the feminine symbol in the underlying resources of humanity, such notions are held to the exclusion of a balancing imagery, resulting in heresy. The word "heresy" is the opposite of the word "catholic," and means to choose one dimension of the available meaning of God as opposed to another.[12] The Catholic faith is one that expresses the whole possible meaning. The denial of the feminine in ourselves and in the understanding of the experience of God makes such wholeness impossible. It is time that those who appeal to the obsessively narrow-minded grasp of sexuality in Graeco-Roman culture as being "Catholic" realize the one-sidedness of that claim.

The history of Christianity is filled with examples of the underlying feminine symbol attempting to break through this cultural repression, which the church tragically confused with the revealed word of God. The brief identification of the Holy

Spirit as "she," the "underground mythology" surrounding Mary Magdelene (recently appearing in the most lovely of the songs in *Jesus Christ, Superstar*), the twelfth century "courts of love," the cult of the Blessed Virgin, and the matriarchal monastic conventicles are examples. If they sometimes took on pathological dimensions, such as the spontaneous cruelty of medieval man, this is because repressed needs often do. Perhaps the worst "repressers" were the Puritans, whose rigorous and distant God was the most masculine of all, and for them the feminine emerged in its most demonic form: the witch.

It is a moot point whether the ordination of women to the priesthood would be the result, or the cause, or both, of the deterioration of the patriarchal Graeco-Roman culture. This is not a question the Church needs to resolve. What is needed is the realization that the feminine symbol in relation to the masculine symbol needs to find a place in the life and, consequently, the consciousness of the church's understanding of the experience of God. It is time that we cease to suffer the ill effects of the denial that has for two thousand years drawn us into heresy. Perhaps that is strong language, but the proverbial "two-by-four" is needed both for those of us who equate a monochrome cultural experience with the possibilities of God's revelation and for those who do not recognize the deeply embedded power of the symbol of human sexuality.

It would be wrong to ignore the frightening dimensions of the proposal that lies before the church. The masculine understanding of God can make us fearful as one is afraid of the familiar tyrannical father. This is not the kind of terror, however, which we face as we contemplate a God mediated to us by persons who bring into our consciousness the feminine symbol. The God of the Puritans was banal and dull. The God that women priests might conjure up before us will be quite different. Such a God is not familiar; she lives in the darkness of the earth, nurturing and creative. We still do not understand her moods and we cannot predict her ways. She is not the God of the computer, she is the God of the artist. Before her we feel the fright of the unknown that knows no control.

John S. Dunne wrote in A SEARCH FOR GOD IN TIME AND MEMORY that contemporary man will find God in the darkness, not the light of his life.[13] He is speaking of that reduction which results from identifying the self with the light of our learning, not the light of God's presence. His imagery recalls the little child, lying frightened in his dark bedroom, calling out for help. Dunne quotes Paul in saying that we cry out, "Abba," meaning in Aramaic, "Daddy." I know and admire Dunne, but I can only believe he has been seduced by the excessive masculinity of the Apostle. No child I know of, afraid of the dark, calls "Daddy." It is rather "Mama."

NOTES

1 Bernard J. F. Lonergan, S.J., INSIGHT: A STUDY OF HUMAN UNDERSTANDING (3rd ed.; New York: Philosophical Library, 1970), pp. 385 - 387, refers to the underlying problem in all metaphysics of the "polymorphist" nature of human understanding, requiring the dialectical and genetic cognitive process, in which objectivity lies before us and not in our grasp.

2 Urban T. Holmes, THE FUTURE SHAPE OF MINISTRY (New York: Seabury Press, 1971), pp. 8 - 32.

3 Cit. Charles R. Meyer, MAN OF GOD: A STUDY OF THE PRIESTHOOD (Garden City: Doubleday & Company, 1974), p. 138.

4 A further discussion of what I mean by this statement will be found in Robert E. Terwilliger and Urban T. Holmes, eds., TO BE A PRIEST (N.Y.: Seabury Press, 1975).

5 Henri J. M. Nouwen, THE WOUNDED HEALER: MINISTRY IN CONTEMPORARY SOCIETY (Garden City: Doubleday & Company, 1974), pp. 85 - 98.

6 Cit. Jurgen Moltmann, THE CRUCIFIED GOD, (New York: Harper & Row, 1974), p. 6.

7 It would seem to me that this is what Emily C. Hewitt and Suzanne R. Hiatt, WOMEN PRIESTS: YES OR NO (New York: Seabury Press, 1973), p. 44, are saying. The argument that follows suggests that, while the word "difference" conjures up some unfortunate images and should be avoided, the reality of the feminine and masculine symbols are not a matter of indifference.

8 Some will imagine in what I have identified as the "underlying resource" a definite commitment to Jung, since he is so popular now. I would hope that the reader would understand that the term I am using is intentionally vague and avoids Jung's vocabulary because I do not believe the argument rests upon the acceptance or rejection of Jung's theories.

9 Robert E. Ornstein, THE PSYCHOLOGY OF CONSCIOUSNESS (New York: Viking Press, 1972), pp. 50 - 101.

10 Lionel Tiger, MEN IN GROUPS (New York: Random House, 1969) traces the evolution of male bonding from the viewpoint of ethology. It has many implications for the kind of "defensive bonding" I have indicated here.

11 I use this illustration in order to suggest that there is much more to some of our heterosexual manners than mere convention. The obscene is not simply a matter of having a "dirty mind." The obscene relates to the pollution of the incongruous and connotes the ominous that lies within the unknown, powerful, dark, inner drives of man. The word itself means "portentous," "sinister," and is related to the feminine symbol in such a way that one is not "obscene" lightly with the feminine part of our consciousness.

12 The word "catholic" comes from the Greek, *kath holon,* meaning "according

to the whole thing." The Catholic Church is the entire people of God, who take into account all possible truth. A good Catholic would also be a good Protestant, because when we seek to be true to the whole, we become very aware of how partial our sight is and "protest" any identification of historical embodiment of the experience of God with the absolute nature of God *per se.* The word "heretic" comes from the Greek, *haireomai,* meaning "to choose" or "to take for oneself." The word "heretic" has been used in a very cruel way in the history of the Church, and it is understandable why some in the name of tolerance avoid it. However, if we deny the possibility of heresy we lapse into a solipsism, where nothing can be held to be truer than anything else and we are intellectually immobilized. This in its own way is far more tyrannical than the suggestion that heresy does exist.

13 John S. Dunne, A SEARCH FOR GOD IN TIME AND MEMORY (New York: The Macmillan Company, 1969), pp. 113, 176, 192 - 194.

6 Ordination of Women to the Priesthood: Test Case for Anglican Authority

James E. Griffiss

What I propose here is not to argue for the ordination of women to the priesthood and episcopate in the sense of attemptnig to give reasons for doing so. I do not assert that women *ought* to be ordained. Rather I attempt to explore some of the theological questions which are raised by the possibility that the Church may authorize the ordination of women. As will be evident to anyone reading it, the argument is from a fairly conservative point of view. Personally I have some reservations about the advisability of ordaining women, which are not, strictly speaking, theological. At the same time, however, I am convinced that the theological objections which are raised by some opponents are not only groundless but in fact would be very dangerous if used in other areas. They represent a point of view which is not consistent with a sound theological method. My purpose, therefore, is to explore those two areas which are especially important for Anglican theological method: the authority of scripture and tradition, and the eucharistic role of the ordained priest. In so doing, I shall hope to show that if the ordination of women should be permitted by the Church, that action will not represent a fundamental departure from the doctrine and worship of the Episcopal Church, although it would, of course, represent a change in the discipline of the Church. That the Episcopal Church, as an autonomous province of the Anglican Communion, has the authority to make such a change in discipline is without question. Whether it is prudent for us to do so will have to be decided by those having pastoral care for the Church and not by theologians.

— I —

The Anglican Church claims and acknowledges three basic and fundamental sources for its belief and practice: Holy Scripture and tradition, as they are understood and reasonably interpreted. It was the appeal to scripture, tradition, and reason which enabled the Anglican divines to avoid what they saw as the extreme positions of Geneva and Rome at the time of the Reformation, and it has remained a constant theme of Anglican theological method. As Anglicans we have rejected, on the one hand, a fundamentalist view of scripture and tradition and, on the other hand, an infallible magisterium or papacy. We have had to be content with a theological method which cannot lay claim to absolute certainty, but which can only look to patient and reasoned investigation. For that reason we have throughout our history been engaged in what has frequently been a painful voyage of discovery in order to discern what it is that God requires of us as a people. Sometimes we have made mistakes and other times we have followed the truth. But through it all we have had to ask ourselves over and over again what authority do scripture and tradition have for us and how are we to understand and interpret them. More particularly we have had to ask what importance there is for our understanding of scripture and tradition in the scientific, philosophical, and cultural changes which take place in the world. Those changes have frequently affected our understanding of ourselves as a church and have required of us new developments in our understanding of the faith. For that reason, Anglicanism has been more sensitive to changes in society than any other ecclesiastical body.

In our theologcial history it is possible to say that we have generally decided that in our interpretation of scripture and tradition we must be open to two things of great theological importance. First we have recognized that the Holy Spirit works in the world as well as in the church. Because we have had neither an infallible book nor an infallible magisterium, we have not been able to define in a narrow sense how God may choose to direct us, nor have we been able to deny the possible validity of secular currents. They, like everything else, must be patiently and reasonably investigated. Second, we have recognized that all theological speculation must be rooted in the pastoral life of the church. Theological speculation in Anglicanism has always been derived from and directed towards the situation of Christians in the world. It is not insignificant that the best Anglican theology has been written not by academics but by pastors. It has been the *pastoral* problem which has presented the question to the theologian, not the other way around.

These two tendencies in Anglican theology have their weaknesses, and one would not want to suggest that they be universal for other Christian bodies. But they have been our particular calling in the theological community. As a result we have been required to explore the question of the authority of scripture and tradition in a manner that is peculiarly our own. In the current discussion of the ordination of women that peculiar approach is of great importance, for it can, perhaps, give us a theological freedom which is not at the present time available to other theological traditions.

The basis for our understanding of the authority of scripture and tradition has been our conviction that both give us in different ways a fundamental witness to the historic life, death, and resurrection of Christ. Their authority is that to which they witness — Christ himself; they are the words which Christian people have spoken about the Word of God and the deeds which they have done in his name. As such they must be evaluated, understood, and interpreted by the church in every time and place. This stance is what the greatest of Anglican theologians, Richard Hooker, meant when he talked about reason. Reasonable people must apply themselves to a continuing re-examination of Christian belief and practice.

For us Anglicans, Holy Scripture has a primary and fundamental authority because it is the witness of the apostolic community to the event of Christ. It provides us with the first theological interpretation of Jesus by the church, and with the beginning of the history of the church as it developed after the Lord's resurrection. That priority is its primary authority, and Anglicans have generally insisted that one section or part cannot be interpreted out of its historical context. Because we have seen Holy Scripture as a historical document we have taken seriously the consequences of a scientific investigation of its sources and development. We have, therefore, been able to accept and use theological and historical exegesis in our interpretation of scripture, rather than regarding it as a source for proof-texts or as a developed theological system. For that reason the theological use of Holy Scripture must search out that to which it bears witness in its historical and social context, recognizing its authority not in isolated words or phrases but in the commission given to the church to preach Christ.

— II —

In the matter of the ordination of women, Holy Scripture clearly does not say that women ought to be ordained to the priesthood. Neither does it say that men ought to be ordained to the priesthood. It does, however, provide us with the reasons why we as a church may and must make such historical and theological interpretations. The ordained ministry, as we now know it, has its origin and justification in Holy Scripture, but the structure and exact nature of that ministry is not specifically laid out for us. The ordained ministry developed as the church interpreted the apostolic commission. The ordination of women requires a new insight into some areas of Holy Scripture which we may not have been able to see in the past because we were concerned with other, equally important matters. That has happened to the church on many occasions in the past — the immorality of slavery being the most obvious example. But the principle which is involved for a church which claims to deal with Holy Scripture reasonably is a willingness to re-examine its origins.

For Anglicans, tradition is the witness of an ongoing historical community which has attempted to interpret the Gospel and its own past under the direction of the Holy Spirit. Tradition for us is a living reality — our history as a people. Within it one can discover many different interpretations of the Gospel, but always the continuity of witness to the event of Christ. Since the continuity of tradition, and hence its authority for us, is its witness to Christ, one can find new practices and new doctrinal formulations emerging as the church responded to new situations. We are not required, as some Roman Catholics are, to discover in tradition the consistent teaching of an infallible papacy. Tradition is not simply what has always been done. It is rather the history of the interpretation of the event of Christ. Like Holy Scripture, tradition does not give us a specific set of rules which we can apply to every situation which confronts us.

Nor does it give us a set of final theological propositions. What it gives us is the historical interpretation of Jesus Christ as the community has believed in him. It was on this basis that the great ecumenical councils could attempt to restate and redefine the doctrine of Christ for a new situation. The fathers of the councils departed from biblical categories and language, and they gave greater emphasis to certain traditional interpretations of Jesus, as they attempted to express the nature of their belief for a world that was radically different from that of first century Palestine. In doing this they believed themselves consistent with the intention of scripture while at the same time accepting legitimate development in the theological understanding of Christ. The continuity of tradition, as is also true of Holy Scripture, is Christ himself, who is at the center of both. Since he is himself, as we believe, a radically new event in history and one who makes all things new, we must be cautious, at the very least, about saying that the church can never do what has not been done before. That would not be tradition, but rather idolatry of the past.

The tradition does not provide us with any reasonable evidence that requires women to be ordained. It does provide us with a custom of long standing that they should not be. The question which must now be decided by the church is whether that custom should be abandoned and a new development in the tradition recognized. For Anglicans, the basis for making such a decision must be rooted in the pastoral life of the church. If the pastoral life of the church seems to be requiring the priestly ministry of women (as many argue), then the ordained ministry of the church should take that form which enables it to fulfill its apostolic commission in this time and place. Obedience to this commission is what faithfulness to tradition means — not only for this issue but for any other which may arise in the future.

What has been said about Anglican theological method and the authority of scripture and tradition does not, however, meet the major question raised by the possibility that women may be ordained. Ordination to the priesthood involves the particular action of presiding at the eucharist, the action most characteristic of the ordained priesthood as we know it in the church today. And for many people that action is the area of greatest difficulty. Many within the church are strongly opposed to the ordination of women because they believe that the ordained priest, especially in his sacramental function, necessarily represents the maleness of Christ. They would understand the ordained priest as *alter Christus,* another Christ, and therefore they believe that the admission of women into the ordained priesthood would radically alter what we must believe about the human nature of Christ and about the eucharist itself.

There is no denying that such an understanding of the ordained priesthood is one of longstanding. Even though such a doctrine is not mentioned in the New Testament, like so many other beliefs and practices it has its roots in the New Testament. It began to appear in the tradition with some of the Fathers, especially in regard to the bishop as the one who represented the fatherhood of God. As the church's understanding of the eucharist changed and as the ordained priest at the eucharist came more and more to stand for Christ rather than to preside over the assembly, the notion of the priest as *alter Christus* became in the middle ages an ordinary part of the piety surrounding the eucharist. The priest came to represent Christ to the people as he re-enacted the sacrifice of Christ. Such a development was, I believe, perfectly legitimate, and it has been deeply influential in the piety of many people.

Our present task, however, is to ask ourselves whether that particular development of the ordained priest as *alter Christus* is essentially and dogmatically linked to the doctrine of the eucharist and of the ordained prisethood. If it is not, then of course a further development can legitimately take place in our interpretation of scripture and tradition. My belief, to put it briefly, is that if we examine the tradition carefully we shall discover that much of our thinking and our feeling about the ordained priesthood derives not from Holy Scripture nor even from the tradition, but from post-tridentine Roman Catholic piety — a piety which presently many Roman Catholics themselves no longer find adequate. If we examine the sources, we may discover the truth of a remark made by C. S. Lewis, that those who do not know their history are frequently enslaved to a fairly recent past.

The scientific and critical investigation of early Christianity shows us one thing quite clearly: that ecclesial institutions were very fluid at the beginning of the church's history.[1] No one pattern at first existed, but finally a definite pattern did emerge. For the early church, as for us today, the intention of Christ for his church became clear not from his specific words, but from the way in which the church pastorally interpreted his death and resurrection and its own apostolic commission to preach the Gospel. The underlying paradigm for the church in the development of its institutions was the mystery of salvation in Christ. In regard to Holy Orders this pattern is particularly clear. Apparently most of the early local churches were led and governed by a presbytery, one of whose members gradually took oversight of the community through his function of presiding at the eucharist. These leaders became what we now call bishops. The other early order which emerged was the diaconate. It gradually lost its significance until the pastoral need of the church caused its revival in this century. The order of priesthood, as we now know it, is not referred to in the New Testament; it only developed when a bishop delegated to another presbyter the authority to preside at the eucharist. The order of priesthood thus emerged as a distinct office in the church, but it was an office which, like the episcopate and the diaconate, existed within the church, not apart from it. It was an office which was exercised with the whole or general priesthood of the people of God — the *laos*. The priesthood of the church was constituted by baptism. Hence the ordained priesthood was not opposed to the general, baptismal priesthood and it did not diminish the priestly character of the whole church in baptism. Rather it served then, as it must now, for the historical realization and focus of the priesthood of God's people.

— III —

From this brief survey of the development of the institutional ministry, there are three conclusions which can be drawn because of their importance for the question now facing the Church.

1. The priesthood of the church is fundamentally the priesthood of the Christ who in his humanity offers himself to God. The priesthood of the church is bestowed in baptism upon every baptized person, for that is the sacrament of Christian vocation. The priesthood of the church is sacramentally focused and made concrete in the bishop and the presbyters who have oversight and who represent the community before God; but what is focused in them is the priesthood of the whole church. The ordained priesthood, as it has developed over the centuries, is a cultic office of the church's baptismal priesthood. It is, then,

correct to speak of the priesthood of all believers, as Martin
Luther did at the time of the Reformation. It is this general
priesthood which is focused in the ordained priesthood. Martin
Luther, however, was wrong in concluding, as he did, that therefore a cultic order of priesthood is not necessary for the Church
since every baptized person is a priest. But the reason why he
drew such a conclusion is very pertinent not only to our history
as Anglicans but also to our present concern.

2. By the time of the Reformation something of fundamental importance about the order of priesthood had been lost sight
of in the tradition due to social and political conditions and the
development of the idea of priest as *alter Christus*. The priesthood
of the whole church had been supplanted by the priesthood of
the ordained priest. So Luther's protest was right even if his conclusions were wrong. He concluded that the priesthood stood
between the laity and God, and as such should be abolished. On
the contrary, however, what we can now see more clearly is that
it is the priesthood of the whole church through its baptized
members which offers the eucharistic sacrifice, not just the ordained priest alone. The ordained priest is the sacramental focus
of the priesthood of the Church. He does not stand at the altar
by himself but with the people of God. Indeed he is *alter Christus*, but he is such with the laity through his baptism, not apart
from it and not by himself alone. Every Christian is an *alter
Christus;* every Christian is the tangible representation of the
priesthood of Christ through baptism into Christ. Therefore the
ordained priesthood does not stand between the laity and God,
but it stands with the laity in its offering and recalling of the
sacrifice of Christ. Within the body of the Church, which as a
whole images Christ, there is a hierarchy of order, but it is a
pastoral hierarchy of service not of gender, for the Church in its
priesthood includes all baptized people.

3. But, Christ himself was a male. Does that say anything
about the ordained priesthood? In fact it says more about the
doctrine of Christ than it does about the cultic office of the ordained priesthood. Jesus was a male and a Jew; that is the par-
ticularity and concreteness of the Incarnation. For the Judaism
into which he was born, maleness and jewishness were equally
important, because those represent the two basic categories
through which, for the Old Testament, human beings can be
understood. They are either Jew or gentile, male or female. But
we believe that Jesus Christ in his sacrifice on the cross and in

his resurrection include all categories — both Jew and gentile, both male and female — because he establishes a new humanity. And we believe we are doing that very thing when we incorporate human beings into Christ in baptism. Christ is not only a man and a Jew; he is the Man in whom men and women, Jew and gentile, are united to God through his high priesthood.

To say anything less would not be faithful to the catholic tradition as it was stated in the ecumenical creeds and in other early christological formulations. When the church reflected upon the mystery of the Incarnation and when it attempted to state its belief in theological terms, it recognized that the humanity of Christ cannot be identified exclusively with jewishness or maleness. The ecumenical creeds speak always of Christ not as male but as man. While this distinction is obscured for us in English, it is obvious in the Greek language of the creed. Christ is spoken of as *anthropos*, a term which points beyond the distinction of male and female, rather than as *aner*, the term which is used in the particular sense of a male. This is not to say the Fathers were anticipating some contemporary theories about androgyny. It is rather to say that the risen Lord creates a new and redeemed humanity which incorporates all of those distinctions which distinguish human beings from one another. The distinctions are incorporated into his priesthood, that priesthood in which the church shares through baptism. It is therefore theologically necessary to say that Jesus in his perfect and full humanity — in his person as the God-Man — is imaged in both male and female, in both Jew and gentile. Whoever presides at the eucharist can image Christ as the *Anthropos* of God in whom all humanity is redeemed.

There is, I believe, no more reason for saying that the priesthood of Christ cannot be sacramentally focused through a woman than for saying it cannot be sacramentally focused through a gentile. The church, as it responded to its apostolic commission, early decided that in order to be a Christian one did not have to be a Jew. We read the debate in the Book of Acts. The victory which St. Paul won over the other apostles was in its own way a very radical one, even though it may not appear so to us after nineteen hundred years. It represented a significant departure from the tradition of Judaism which had restricted the covenant between God and man to those who were the descendants of Abraham. Paul saw that God's saving work in

Christ extended to all human beings, not just to the Jews, and that all human beings could be incorporated into Christ through baptism. As has so often happened in the past, it may well be that the Holy Spirit at work in the world and new pastoral needs within the community are enabling the Church to see one aspect of scripture and tradition in a new way. Both scripture and tradition are living because they witness to the one who is Lord of all history and all time, and it is possible that the Holy Spirit may lead us into new ways of understanding them.

As I said at the beginning of this paper, there are many practical and prudential questions which must be resolved if the Episcopal Church is to allow the ordination of women to the priesthood and episcopate. But I do believe that, if the Church should decide to do so, it will be a legitimate development within catholic tradition — a new thing, yes, but a development which has its foundation in the only foundation which the Christian community can have, namely, in the mystery of Christ himself. Only the Holy Spirit will show us finally whether we have followed truth. It is important, however, for Anglicans to remember that we began our ecclesiastical history with just such a doubt when we separated ourselves from much custom, piety, and tradition at the time of the Reformation. If we believe that the Holy Spirit has guided this Church into a richer appreciation of its catholic heritage during the past five hundred years, then I see no reason for thinking that we shall be deserted now.

NOTES

1 There are many studies of the origins of the ministerial office in the New Testament. The most readily available is Raymond E. Brown, PRIEST AND BISHOP (New York: 1970).

2 Again the most readily available edition of the Latin and Greek texts of the Ecumenical Creeds is Philip Schaff, THE CREEDS OF CHRISTENDOM, Vol. II (New York: 1896).

7 Patriarchy and the Ordination of Women

Ruth Tiffany Barnhouse

There is an enormous concern, particularly in Anglo-Catholic circles, lest the ordination of women to the priesthood disturb in some unacceptably profane way our essential relationship to the sacred mysteries. In a previous paper I attempted to show that the arguments against women's ordination based on the masculinity of God founder on the demonstration of God's androgyny. This is particularly evident in the Genesis creation story:

> Let us make man in our own image, in the likeness of ourselves . . . God created man in the image of himself, in the image of God he created him, male and female he created them.[1]

Further, I attempted to show that the symbolism of the eucharist is multivalent, and clearly includes feminine elements at all levels. By limiting its enactment to male celebrants, we are depriving ourselves of the opportunity to experience an important aspect of its significance.[2]

In this paper I propose to deal with the institution of patriarchy which I agree is threatened by the ordination of women. I shall consider it in terms of the evolution of consciousness, and shall attempt to show that its passing is to be applauded, not mourned. I shall also attempt to show that serious perils await us if we permit secular forces to preside over its dissolution. I hope to demonstrate the reasons why the church should take the lead in this profound change. Finally, I shall explain why I believe this can and must be accomplished without doing violence to the Christian tradition.

— I —

The mysteries are carried in our myths and in our liturgies. Since the word myth is used to mean so many different things, let me begin by explaining the precise sense in which I use it. It does not mean that which is unreal, fictional, or untrue. On the contrary, a myth is *more* true than any rational statement could possibly hope to be. This is because rational statements are designed by the human intellect, and are tailored to suit its limitations. They generally attempt to be unambiguous, non-paradoxical, and comprehensible *from the human point of view*. Truth, on the other hand, and most especially the divine truths which religion attempts to grasp, is entirely independent of these human intellectual limitations. From the human point of view truth is often paradoxical, ambiguous and unclear, fraught with mystery, and a serious stumbling-block to our intellectual pride. As Father Capon has said:

> The Mystery — remaining steadfastly and stubbornly mysterious — must always be seen as governing the images. What we *mean* by the word God, for example, is not what God *is;* it is a tentative handle by which, at best, we give ourselves some slight and mitten-handed feel of the heft of the reality. Again, *Hypostasis* is not the full measure of Father, Son, and Spirit in their distinction, but simply an agreed upon way of talking — a word which, in a certain historical and cultural setting was made to sit still long enough to do a particular piece of theological dog-work.[3]

This Mystery has been given us primarily (though perhaps not exclusively) through our sacred myths.

Sacred myths function in many ways, perhaps the most important of which is to maintain synthesis, or sense of wholeness, in the face of terms which to the conscious rationality would present either intellectual or emotional difficulties, or both. Taking for granted that the source of truth is God, and that he is active in attempting to convey it to us, it has been amply demonstrated, most recently and thoroughly by Carl Jung, that the human receptor organ for revelation and inspiration is that part of our psyche which is unconscious, non-rational. (*Non-rational* is to be distinguished from *irrational*.) God has spoken to us in dreams, in visions, in unique encounters with individuals. The meeting with God is always a total experience for the one who meets him. Typically God appears to the prophet, the apostle, the saint (or, for that matter, to the person-in-the-street), in an archetypally mysterious way. It is after this encounter that rational consciousness comes into play, and is used by the prophets, saints, and apostles to try to mediate their experience to the community at large in intellectually comprehensible terms. This communication is at the very least difficult, and sometimes impossible. Until very recently, and perhaps largely even now if the truth were told, most people relate to religion through myths and symbols principally expressed in cultic observance, and not through their rational mind. As St. Paul and others following him have never wearied of telling us, God is not encountered through the exercise of the intellect, but by grace, through mysterious operations of the Spirit.

— II —

Consciousness, like every other part of the universe, is in a continuing state of evolution. It is easy to assent to this proposition, but very difficult to grasp what it really entails. The modern theory of evolution arose in the heyday of nineteenth-century deterministic materialism, at a time when it was believed that sufficient energetic application of the empirical scientific method would eventually reveal that everything is reducible to its physical components, even religious experience. This led to an exacerbation of dualism, or the gnostic heresy in modern dress. The Gnostics held that matter was an evil illusion whereas science was to hold, and for the most part still does, that spirit is a foolish illusion.[4] As Christians we must reject both of these views. But the only way to stay out of them and retain our intellectual integrity is to recognize that acceptance of the biological evolution necessarily implies spiritual evolution as well. God's truths may indeed be eternal and to some extent totally beyond our grasp, but our ability partially to perceive them and our perforce limited understanding of such as we do perceive is always conditioned by the state of development of our consciousness. An obvious result of this is that as consciousness evolves, truths that could formerly only be held in their mythical form become gradually more comprehensible in abstract and rational terms. That which appeared paradoxical to the primitive mind at the dawn of the race may now be part of the everyday knowledge of the human child.

The theologian's task is to interpret the myths, which is in some sense always to demythologize them. The overdevelopment and overvaluation of rational abstract understanding in our day has frequently led to premature demythologizing. This can have no result other than an iconoclastic one. By the time that the myth or symbol has been reduced to elements which can be fully grasped by the rational consciousness, much of value has been lost or discarded.

Those who perceive themselves as among the few who truly value the cultic life feel that it is designed to preserve the mysteries and sacralize daily existence. It is thus the carrier of their daily life. It is not surprising that they should vigorously resist attempts to tamper with these mysteries and symbols. It is also not surprising that they should, at least initially, preceive the movement furthering the ordination of women in this light.

The formulations of theologians are essentially conditional, depending as they do on limitations of intellect as well as on historical and cultural determinants. Bearing this fact in mind, let us attempt to re-examine the cultic observances which have evolved over the centuries for the purpose of bringing the meaning of the sacred myths into the living experience of believers. We shall do so in the hope that they may shed some new light on the question of patriarchy.

In a previous paper I examined the symbolism of the eucharist to show that it is a rite of individuation for all human beings, and therefore is independent of the patriarchal system.[5] The available anthropological and historical evidence suggests that patriarchy is a human cultural form, not a divinely appointed eternal foundation of human society. Since our sacred scriptures were written during the patriarchal period, it is to be expected that they should reflect that fact. If sufficiently good reasons appear, however, we do not need to be bound to that social structure simply because it appears in scripture, any more than we need to believe in seven twenty-four-hour-days of creation, or take literally the injunction to pluck out our right eye if it offends us. But I part company with those who would now engage in the rather futile exercise of condemning patriarchy out of hand, declaring that it has always been at least oppressive, if not actually evil. On the contrary, I assume that it was a neces-sary stage in the evolution of human consciousness. In that case, its temporary existence *is* part of the divine plan, and it has brought much of great value to both men and women in its time.

— III —

Let us consider this idea in more detail. There is a general evolutionary principle which states that ontogeny recapitulates phylogeny. Let us assume that this holds true not only for bio-logical development but also for the development of conscious-ness. Further, biological evolution and the evolution of con-sciousness both proceed in two ways, one of which is gradual and the other relatively sudden. The gradual mode in both instances is that brought about by the slow shaping of the ecological sys-tems of nature on the one hand, and of community and cultural force on the other. In biology the sudden mode is that of muta-tion, which is sometimes discontinuous with and antagonistic to what has gone before, and is therefore lethal to the species or individual involved. At other times it produces growth and de-velopment in new and constructive directions. With respect to consciousness, the psychological experience of revelation or in-spiration produces sudden effects. Fallen humanity is all too expert at listening to the false voices of its own idols, and nu-minous encounters with the demonic cosmic forces are not un-known. Following these messages leads to havoc and disorder — sometimes even to mass regression. But the true revelations of God can also produce a great leap forward in the eschatological direction of the ultimate divine plan. This may happen in the spiritual pilgrimage of one person, or it may affect an entire civilization.

With these ideas in mind, let us see what we may learn about the racial evolution of consciousness by considering the psychological process through which a child grows from infancy to maturity. At first the infant is not aware of the distinction between self and others in the environment, but is locked in a symbiotic relationship with the mother. This corresponds to the primitive cultural state of *participation mystique*. Here the in-dividual symbiosis with the mother is projected onto the envi-ronment, and the members of the group experience themselves in a similar symbiotic relationship with nature. Dixon describes the religion of this prehistoric (and probably matriarchal) period as "... fertility cults where the women (therefore the men) were natural functions and not persons."[6] Life in such primitive societies is almost entirely collective. Individuals experience themselves and one another in terms of their role in the society and not in terms of their own unique personal psychological development.

As human infants continue to develop, there is a gradual process of differentiation in which they come to recognize themselves as separate persons. It is important to note that the person from whom it is most urgent that they become separate is the mother, since it is with her that the original symbiosis occurs. The most basic step in the long process of separation from the mother is the recognition of the father. It is no doubt for this reason that the corresponding period in the development of human consciousness was characterized by the gradual development of patriarchal culture. In this view, patriarchy was a necessary condition for the emergence of human consciousness from the original symbiosis with "Mother Nature." It is important to note that patriarchy arose in numerous polytheistic cultures, and is not, even in the West, a result of the rise of monotheism.

After infancy has been successfully negotiated, and the first stages of separation from the mother achieved, comes childhood, the period in which the rules of civilized behavior are learned. The concept of responsibility is grasped, beginning with the lesson that one is accountable to others for one's actions. This process is accomplished by gradually acquainting children with rules and with the consequences which will ensue if they are broken. Such training is usually resisted to a greater or lesser degree, but is tolerated because of the increments of freedom which it brings.

On the larger scale of the development of consciousness it will be seen at once how the process thus far described corresponds to that which is illustrated in the early myths of the Old Testament. Abraham was called forth and informed of his uniqueness, of his differentiation from the general group of humanity. It would be too time-consuming to go through the history of his descendants point by point, but suffice it to say that in the story of Moses receiving the tables of the Law we have the culmination of this part of the process. It was through the Law that the idea of individual responsibility was thoroughly inculcated and the process of individual differentiation carried out. Nevertheless, this stage is far from representative of full human maturity. Although individuals are no longer lost in a symbiotic relationship with nature or the feminine maternal principle, they are still heavily dependent on the community standards of the patriarchal tribe or nation. The exercise of conscience at this stage does not consist in determining for oneself what is right, but in determining whether one has obeyed to the best of one's ability the laws imposed by a higher authority.

When childhood is over, the individual passes into adolescence. The salient indispensable feature of this stage is the physiological development of sexuality and the psychological growth required to assimilate it. With adolescence comes the possibility, but not the absolute necessity, of going on to full psychological and spiritual maturity. Jung summarizes the development up to this point as follows:

> Undoubtedly the personalities of father and mother form the first and apparently the only world of man as an infant; and, if they continue to do so for too long, he is on the surest road to neurosis, because the great world he will have to enter as a whole person is no longer a world of fathers and mothers, but a supra-personal fact. The child first begins to wean itself from the childhood relation to father and mother through its relation to its brothers and sisters. . . . Later, husband and wife are originally strangers to one another. . . . When children come, they complete the process by forcing the parents into the role of father and mother, which the parents, in accordance with their infantile attitude, formerly saw only in others, thereby trying to secure for themselves all the advantages of the childhood role. Every more or less normal life runs this enantiodromian course and compels a change of attitude from the extreme of the child to the other extreme of the parent.[7]

— IV —

It is evident that within social organization as it has existed up to now, it is entirely possible for people to live out their whole lives without going beyond this stage of incorporating the received value system of the patriarchal society. At any time in human history it is clear that the great majority of individual human beings lead a fundamentally collective existence, conditioned as that may be by the ideals and standards developed by those articulate and relatively well educated persons, (overwhelmingly male under patriarchy), who are in the effective vanguard of the evolutionary process.

But this last thought is not offered in support of any elitist philosophy. There have always been individuals, however bound by the social structures and community standards of their time, who have perfected and matured their psyche in harmonious cooperation of heart, soul, mind and strength. Such people are not necessarily visible in the noisy crowd doing most of the writing, talking and decision-making in the marketplace. Their spiritual achievement is seldom brought to our educated notice. In fact, we might be arrogantly tempted to dismiss this idea as a romantic fantasy were it not for such contemporary documentation as that provided by Robert Coles in his moving essay "A New Heaven and a New Earth."[8] Reading this work should bring the gift of humble tears even to those most confirmed in intellectual and spiritual pride.

Nevertheless, it was not until the seventeenth century that the idea of the supremacy of individual conscience over the community's view of "truth" began to take public hold on a large scale. (As I shall attempt to show, this change was the first symptom of the terminal illness of the patriarchal system.) Prior to that time, the educated religious authorities had always presided over basic changes in consciousness. How did the church lose its initiative in this matter? I believe that the loss occurred as a result of the very mistaken premises on which the church waged its famous battle with science. It made the serious if understandable error of not recognizing the true character of the sacred myths, and therefore interpreted them too literally. It failed to distinguish between the provisional, humanly conditioned understanding of those myths and their ultimate meaning. It appears to me crucial that this error not be repeated now that the church confronts the sociological revolution which is involved in the decline of patriarchy. Were that repetition to occur, it would not only be a failure of nerve, but more importantly a failure of faith. In order to appreciate the vastness and subtlety of the scale, both spatial and temporal, subjective and objective, in which the drama of evolution is unfolding, it is necessary to appreciate the developments not only in physics, astronomy and biology, but also in depth psychology. Although such dimensions were hardly suspected by any of the human authors of Holy Writ through whom God communicated with mankind, this scale and these dimensions have of course always been known to God himself. We must have faith that if we examine the myths aright, we will find in them clear guidelines on how to play our part in the next act of God's drama. If we fail to do so, we will not hold back the course of history or of social evolution. We will merely allow the secular arm of society, which is concerned with short-term "practical" benefits only, usually of a selfish and hedonistic character, to plunge us into a Dark Age of destructive regression. This is inevitable, because secular values are not eternal. They focus on less than the divine, and are therefore always idolatrous.

A little thought will show that full personal maturity requires development of conscience beyond the stage of responsibility to uphold the received standards of family, tribe, nation — or church. In short, it requires the kind of development the potential for which was ushered in by the Incarnation. The life and teachings of Jesus make it clear that he was offering to mankind a liberation from the Old Law, and a freedom which, to the rulers of the time, had the appearance of anarchy. What he was proposing was full, individual responsibility of each person directly to God. Jung describes this change:

> Nevertheless, it was the great and imperishable achievement of Christianity that, in contrast to these archaic systems which are all based on the original projection of psychic contents, it gave to each individual man the dignity of an immortal soul, whereas in earlier times this prerogative was reserved to the sole person of the king. . . . The innate will to consciousness, to moral freedom and culture, proved stronger than the brute compulsion of projections which keep the individual permanently imprisoned in the dark of unconsciousness and grind him down into nonentity.[9]

Naturally such a radical transcendent vision could not take root overnight and give rise immediately to new cultural forms. It is therefore not surprising that patriarchy continued to be the prevailing cultural pattern within which Christian traditions were developed, particularly after the mixed blessing of Christianity's becoming the state religion following Constantine's conversion. But it is worth noting that a dispassionate examination of the teachings of Jesus does not reveal any divine ground for perpetuating the human institution of patriarchy for its own sake beyond such time as it has outlived its usefulness.

All of his utterances were designed to lead listeners to a richer and deeper dimension of consciousness than was indicated by the Mosaic Law. In the terminology of Jesus, the Kingdom of God was not to be described by the social and legal conditions of the eschatological community, but by the individual spiritual maturity of the participants. The desperately high standard of self-examination which he proposed was not designed to increase our burden of guilt, though it has all too often been used that way over the centuries by legalists who failed to understand that what he was really trying to tell us is that the fullest possible extension of individual consciousness is the path to the true freedom in God. He was mounting a major assault on the collective mode of being. He took for granted that women were to be included as independent participants in the Kingdom, and this made him a radical feminist in the cultural context of his time.[10] It was Milton misinterpreting St. Paul, and not Jesus himself, who said, ". . . he for God, she for God in him."

It is not therefore surprising that, despite some current rhetoric to the contrary, the position of women in Christianity greatly improved over what it had been in pagan times. Not only was this true in society generally, but also within the church. As Eleanor McLaughlin has shown, throughout the Middle Ages holiness was not considered to be contingent on sex. During that time the patriarchal structure was limited to the institutional organization of the church, and did not extend to the realm of personal spiritual development; nor did it inhibit the public influence of saintly believers who happened to be women.[11] This illustrates the important point that even when patriarchy is very strong, that does not necessarily imply oppression of women. It depends entirely on how it is implemented, what corresponding position women are put in, what corresponding responsibilities and dignities they have. It was, after all, the patriarchal period that produced the proverb: "The hand that rocks the cradle rules the world." Things work best in a culture when the masculine and feminine principles are more or less equally conscious, and more or less equally developed.[12] The higher Christian standard of the full and separate individuation of each person means that the projections must be withdrawn, and that the native androgyny of the human psyche must come into conscious play. Individuals must become aware of the contrasexual element of their own psyche and make friends with it, indeed, they must form a partnership with it. It will no longer suffice to define one's own gender identity by conspicuously avoiding those traits traditionally associated with the opposite sex. One must now discover the full range of who one really is.

— V —

In a more collective cultural organization, it works perfectly well for most people to be unconscious of their own contrasexual component and to allow that to be projected onto the members of the group who are in fact of the opposite sex. But in a society where, for whatever reasons, one sex is defined as hierarchically superior to the other, this kind of group projection will result in the qualities and principles of the secondary sex, *however valuable and even actually valued they may be,* being developed only in subsidiary relation to the values and qualities of the dominant sex, and will therefore remain largely unconscious and unarticulated. They will not have a chance to be developed independently, or on their own terms. Eventually, even though this may not be obvious for a long period of time, full individuation of the secondary sex will be thwarted.

This is just the situation of which we are now, in the last hundred years, suddenly conscious. This is because evolution has proceeded to the point where people are aware for the first time of something which they have taken for granted for thousands of years. They are beginning to experience the consequences of the fact that up to now the assignment of sexual roles in society has rested very greatly on unconscious projections. The reason the current confrontation is so painful is that the development of masculine values has gotten out of hand. Now in the consciousness of the twentieth century, we have a dangerous overplus of the masculine principle. It has been far more highly developed and far more sophisticatedly elaborated than the feminine principle, and this has been going on for several hundred years. The Enlightenment, with its emphasis on formal logic, pure reason, and "objective" empirical science, and the Reformation with its iconoclasm, culminating in such things as the quest for the historical Jesus and the emphasis on *logos, kerygma,* and "God acting in history," have left the feminine principle pretty far behind. Women are of course not the only ones to have been seriously deprived by these developments.

This result happened because when the supremacy of individual conscience began to be recognized in the seventeenth century, and during the ensuing period when the idea of individual rights and freedom began to flower, it was not recognized that in the long run these values would prove incompatible with patriarchy. The attempt to pursue individualism while simultaneously retaining patriarchy could only result in the refinement of the male conscience to a degree outstripping that permitted to the female, (which may be why Freud thought women were less moral than men), and the unbalanced, inadequately compensated development of other masculine values.

Because of the inexorable processes of growth, the old cultural clothes are too tight, they just do not fit anymore. There is no longer room for the fullest development even of men, let alone women, in the old framework. It is extremely significant that each wave of the feminist movement has had men in its vanguard: John Stuart Mill in the last century, followed in this one by the decision of the majority of men to give women the vote. Currently, every sane line of thought which has been proposed by the women's liberation movement was anticipated by Ashley Montagu, whose book, THE NATURAL SUPERIORITY OF WOMEN, was published in 1952, although portions of it appeared in magazines as early as 1945. Simone de Beauvoir's THE SECOND SEX did not appear in English until 1953 (French edition 1949), and Betty Friedan's THE FEMININE MYSTIQUE was not published until 1963.

As early as 1958, in an article entitled "The Crisis of American Masculinity," Arthur Schlesinger wrote:

... the key to the recovery of masculinity does not lie in any wistful hope of humiliating the aggressive female and restoring the old masculine supremacy. Masculine supremacy, like white supremacy, was the neurosis of an immature society. It is good for men as well as for women that women have been set free ... For the nineteenth-century sense of masculinity was based on the psychological idealization and the legal subjection of women; masculinity so superiously derived could never — and should never — have endured. The male had to learn to live at some point with the free and equal female.[13]

— VI —

If we go on to consider the psychological significance of the rise of the secular state and totalitarianism, we will see that the fate which awaits us if we look back over our shoulder longing for the old patriarchy is far worse than merely turning into a pillar of salt. In 1941, surveying the chaos that was Europe, Jung wrote:

And just as the Church was once absolute in its determination to make theocracy a reality, so the State is now making an absolute bid for totalitarianism. The mystique of the spirit . . . (has been replaced) . . . by the total incorporation of the individual in a political collective called the "State." This offers a way out of the dilemma, for the parental imagos can now be projected upon the State as the universal provider and the authority responsible for all thinking and willing. The ends of science are made to serve the social collective and are only valued for their practical utility to the collective's ends. The natural course of psychological development is succeeded, not by a spiritual direction which spans the centuries and keeps cultural values alive, but by a political directorate which ministers to the power struggles of special groups and promises economic benefits to the masses.[14]

He goes on to point out how painful and difficult the process of individuation always is. Anyone who has ever raised children knows how hard it is to persuade them to take each successive step to maturity. This is never accomplished without tears and struggle. This fact is reflected in the popular, romantic view of childhood as a time of innocence and happiness, and one hears it said, "Isn't it a shame that they have to grow up!" To spare their children this pain is the thoughtless loving motive behind the disastrous child-rearing practices of over-protective parents. But when it is time for the elevation of group consciousness in order to effect a general increment of maturity, the task becomes immeasurably more difficult. About this Jung says:

. . . it can be accomplished, if at all, only by stages, century by century, and it must be paid for by endless suffering and toil in the struggle against all those powers which are incessantly at work persuading us to take the apparently easier road of unconsciousness. Those who go the way of unconsciousness imagine that the task can safely be left to "others" . . . .[14]

And it is not only Jung who calls attention to this aspect of the problem. As long ago as the 1830's de Tocqueville perceived that the "tyranny of the majority" was the soft underbelly of democracy.

Even though we in the United States do not live under a politically totalitarian regime, we have recently had the sobering experience of the most extensive scandal in high places in the history of our government, brought about by a demonic lust for power on the part of men who lacked any semblance of integrity or principle. It *could* happen here. But although we have escaped open political tyranny, we have become victims, more than any other people in the world, of the tyranny of the marketplace. The advertising industry, supported by the professional expertise of psychologists and anthropologists, has seduced us into giving up our spiritual birthright for a mess of consumer goods. While our attention was distracted by the equivalent of pretty beads for the stupid natives, the lies were whispered in our ear so often that we no longer realize that what is good for General Motors is *not* good for the country. In a recent book, Professor Key has described in terrifing and disgusting detail the lengths to which subliminal stimulation of unconscious primitive fears and instincts has been carried from purely commercial motives.[16] To maximize the pay-off to the exploiters, it is necessary to have a significant segment of the society whose principal task is to be consumers. Middle-class women were the natural choice to fill this role, which very soon began to create in them the first symptoms of the psychological malaise that eventually erupted in the women's liberation movement. Although she devotes a whole chapter of THE FEMININE MYSTIQUE to this cynical manipulation, I believe that Betty Friedan underestimated the causal importance of this factor to the social problem she was describing.[17] The occasionally reckless battle cry of various kinds of metaphorical rape by vocal proponents of women's liberation really applies here.

But this catalog of horrors perpetrated by the individualistic male patriarchy, inadequately balanced either by religion or by strong feminine values, includes not only the sins of business but of technology. In a recent book, AT THE EDGE OF HISTORY, William Thompson, who is a former humanities professor at MIT, says:

The phallic culture of our industrial civilization begins with the toy guns of little boys, develops into the puberty rites of car and motorcycle, and climaxes in the technological rape of Vietnam. But, of course, we are told by our behavioral scientists whose research is financed by the government, all these things are separate and unrelated. The family life of engineer, the fantasies of adolescent men, the sexuality of advertising, all these have nothing to do with the whole technological culture of America. . . . the instinctive play of our technology is the exploitation of passive, female nature in a celebration of power and phallic dominance. In keeping with this sexual mythology of rational male dominance over irrational female nature, we have constructed an ideology of progress that places our industrial culture at the pinnacle of human civilization.[18]

The modern Tower of Babel is nearly complete, and we may expect that God will deal with it no less summarily than he did with the original. When Jung wrote about the state in 1941, he was no doubt thinking of Hitler and Stalin; but as we read it again today in the light of the foregoing, its application to our own situation is very clear:

Exactly *who* is the State? — The agglomeration of all the nonentities composing it. Could it be personified, the result would be an individual, or rather a monster, intellectually and ethically far below the level of most of the individuals in it, since it represents mass psychology raised to the *n*th power. Therefore Christianity in its best days never subscribed to a belief in the State, but set before man a supramundane goal which should redeem him from the compulsive force of his projections upon this world, whose ruler is the spirit of darkness. And it gave him an immortal soul that he might have a fulcrum from which to lift the world off its hinges, showing him that his goal lies not in the mastery of this world, but in the attainments of the Kingdom of God, whose foundations are in his own heart.[19]

— VII —

We saw earlier that patriarchy informed by Christian values had much to recommend it for a time, and this is perhaps the reason why ecclesiastical authorities are among the last to recognize that it is doomed. But if the church persists in being the last stronghold of a patriarchy which, in its extreme secular forms, is well on the way to destroying our civilization, Christianity included, it will not even be a voice crying in the wilderness, but will merely be delivering its own funeral oration. As Jung points out,

> When the political aim predominates . . . a secondary thing has been made the primary thing. Then the individual is cheated out of his rightful destiny and two thousand years of Christian civilization are wiped out.[20]

The time has come for the church to give up its patriarchal nostalgia. It *must* now take an active part in the process of bringing into full function the neglected feminine half of human potential. If we continue to permit the present serious distortion of the *imago dei*, we will gravely hamper our progress toward a better vision of the divine original.

The purely secular modes of improving the position of women in our society are fraught with peril, and contain the seeds of unimaginable disorder and regression. This is true because the consciousness of even those women who are most aware of masculine oppression, and who are therefore most active in opposing it, was in fact shaped and conditioned by the patriarchal system. Many of them either still believe, however unconsciously, in the superiority of the masculine principle, or else they are so out of touch with their own femininity that they are unable to imagine their own full, mature development, independent of masculine values. This has led to an unfortunate tendency to deny that there are any real differences, other than the superficial anatomical ones, between men and women. Needless to say, this view is not opposed by those who have a vested interest in maintaining the supremacy of masculine values.

This is nowhere more evident than in the dangerously growing trend to a polymorphously perverse sexual license which masquerades under the name of freedom. Because they are afraid to insist on their own natural feminine approach to sex, women are unfortunately buying the idea that adoption of the hitherto predominantly male patterns of sexual behavior constitutes an important part of their liberation. While the primary male focus on the physical aspects of sex is essential to the preservation of the race, any mature man who is on good terms with his own *anima* can testify that this is surely intended to be augmented by a more naturally feminine emphasis on the overall state of the relationship between the partners, including its emotional and spiritual aspects.[21]

The clear lesson of history is that the decay of a civilization is always accompanied by a breakdown in sexual morality, and by the decline of religion. Nor do I believe that the coincidence of these phenomena of social deterioration is accidental. The sacraments of the Christian religion translate the participants into eternity by means of a time-bound event, namely, the outward and visible occasion of each particular celebration. It is for this reason (and not in support of patriarchy, as some misguided reformers would have us believe), that marriage is numbered among the sacraments. The divinely inspired author of the Song of Songs heads the list of those who, through the centuries, have understood that sexuality itself is a symbol of wholeness, of the reconciliation of opposites, of the loving at-one-ment between God and Creation. In the word of the great contemporary composer, Olivier Messiaen (who is a devout Roman Catholic), ". . . the union of true lovers is for them a transformation on the cosmic scale."[22] I am not, of course, suggesting a return to the legalistic and guilt-ridden rigidity of the sexual codes of the past. But there is a very real difference between the *evolution* of sexual morality and the *dissolution* which threatens us today.

Even the most ignorant or depraved person is animated by some inchoate, primitive religious instinct. If the church does not throw some healing light on the uncharted landscape before us, we may expect that the golden calves will begin to appear. One of the most frightening possibilities is suggested by John Dixon. Speaking of the urgent need for change in our liturgical life he says:

> The liturgists are not now a guide, which is a tragic omission, *for the liturgy ought to be the principal focus of the construction of the soul.* . . . The use of the resources that are available requires some care, precisely because it is so easy to let them be ways back into the nature cults. Contemporary sexual 'freedom' is more nearly a way either of denying the power and authority of sexuality or of reverting to the fertility cults, precisely because sexuality has no context, no narrative or ritual placement which can make it part of the whole.[23]

Were the fertility cults to return, it would constitute a regressive loss of our painfully acquired responsible consciousness, and it is doubtful that the human family could survive the ensuing Dark Ages. If there are any who do not realize what the religiously uninformed explosion of primitive femininity in angry rebellion against the decaying secular patriarchy would be like, let them strengthen their spirit with prayer and fasting and then read the feminist Shulamith Firestone's serious prescription for the future, THE DIALECTIC OF SEX (Wm Morrow, 1970).

— VIII —

To those who find themselves persuaded by my argument, it will be evident that the church not only should, but *must* ordain women to the priesthood. It must abandon the sinking ship of patriarchy and begin forthwith the construction of a new vessel, one sturdy enough to carry the fragile human spirit closer to the Rock of Ages. By so doing, we will not be changing the meaning of our life-carrying liturgies and sacred myths. But we will be making it possible to contemplate and celebrate them in a new way, one which carries the promise of revealing to us as yet unsuspected depths of meaning, without destroying the continuity of two thousand years of religious experience. Urban Holmes is right when he says that ". . . one way in which Christianity has failed sacramentally is not to tap the powerful orectic symbol of the masculine/feminine interaction," and that if women are ordained ". . . the symbolic effect of the ritual they lead will be different!"[24]

It is intentional that throughout this paper I have used the impersonal pronoun "it" in referring to the church. I fervently hope that soon she will once more become the Mother of us all, and teach us to take part in a loving human community in which what men and women can do *together* for the greater glory of God will far surpass the sum of what they have been able to accomplish separately.

NOTES

1 Gn 1:26 - 27 (Jerusalem Bible).
2 Ruth Tiffany Barnhouse, M.D. "An Examination of the Ordination of Women to the Priesthood in Terms of the Symbolism of the Eucharist," *Anglican Theological Review* 56 (1974), pp. 279 - 291.
3 Robert Farrar Capon, "The Ordination of Women: A Non-Book," *Anglican Theological Review,* Supplementary Series no. 2 (September, 1973), p. 69.
4 Sigmund Freud, THE FUTURE OF AN ILLUSION (Liveright Publishing Corporation, 1949), *passim.* Particularly obvious in this book, but also clear from the rest of his writings, is the fact that Freud's psychology also rests

on this materialistic basis. He believed that ethics could be separated from the *numinosum,* a position which I believe the work of C. G. Jung to have definitively refuted.

5 Barnhouse, "Examination of the Ordination of Women," pp. 289 - 290.

6 John Dixon, "Paradigms of Sexuality," *Anglical Theological Review* 56 (1974), p. 158.

7 Carl C. Jung, "Psychotherapy Today" (1941), COLLECTED WORKS, Bollingen Series (Princeton: Princeton U. Press, 1966), vol. 16, pp. 95 - 96.

8 In Doris Ulmann, THE DARKNESS AND THE LIGHT (Millerton, N.Y.: Aperture, Inc., 1974), pp. 81 - 111.

9 Jung, "Psychotherapy Today," p. 105.

10 For a succinct exposition of this idea, with good references to other authors who have developed it, see Alicia Craig Faxon, WOMEN AND JESUS (Philadelphia: United Church Press, 1973).

11 Eleanor McLaughlin, "The Christian Past: Does It Hold a Future for Women?" *Anglican Theological Review* 57 (1975), pp. 36 - 56.

12 For a fuller discussion of the masculine and feminine principles and the concept of androgyny (*animus/anima*), see Barnhouse, "Examination of the Ordination of Women," pp. 285 - 288.

13 Arthur Schlesinger, Jr., "The Crisis of American Masculinity," *Esquire,* 50, no. 5 (Nov., 1958).

14 Jung, "Psychotherapy Today," p. 104.

15 *Ibid.,* p. 105.

16 Wilson Bryan Key, SUBLIMINAL SEDUCTION (Englewood Cliffs: Prentice-Hall, 1973).

17 Betty Friedan, THE FEMININE MYSTIQUE (N.Y.: W. W. Norton, 1963), chapt. 9, "The Sexual Sell."

18 William Irwin Thompson, AT THE EDGE OF HISTORY (N.Y.: Harper Colophon, 1972), pp. 79 and 82.

19 Jung, "Psychotherapy Today," p. 106.

20 *Ibid.,* p. 107.

21 For a more detailed explanation of the difference between male and female sexuality and of the dangers of modern trends, see Ruth Tiffany Barnhouse, "Sexism in Counseling: Some Theoretical Aspects," *Counseling and Values* 19 (1975): 147 - 154. Ruth Tiffany Barnhouse, "Intimacy and the Spiritual Life," *New Catholic World* 218, no. 1305 (May/June, 1975).

22 Olivier Messaien, "Turangalila Symphony, Notes by the Composer" record jacket (New York: RCA: LSC-7051, 1968).

23 Dixon, "Paradigms of Sexuality," pp. 157 - 158 (italics mine).

24 Urban T. Holmes, "Priesthood and Sexuality: A Caveat Only Dimly Perceived," *Anglican Theological Review* 55 (1973), p. 67.

8 Ordination of Women? - -
An Ecumenical Meditation and A Discussion

Frans Jozef van Beeck, S.J.

A Meditation

The worst thing to do is to shrug one's shoulders, for it means you — with your concern — are unimportant. I cannot imagine Jesus shrugging his shoulders. He knew that the Father had entrusted *everything* to him (Jn 13:3). He let everything the Father had given him come to him, and was determined never to turn away anyone who came (Jn 6:37).

That does not mean that Jesus let himself be dominated by the concerns that people brought to him. Recognizing them is not the same as allowing yourself to become enslaved by them. Jesus knew that he had come from God and was going back to God (Jn 13:3). Paul came to know that, too:

> If I am called to account by you or by any human court
> of judgment, it does not matter to me in the least. Why,
> I do not even pass judgment on myself, for I have nothing
> on my conscience; but that does not mean I stand ac-
> quitted. My judge is the Lord (1 Cor 4:3 - 4).

The church is called to share in this freedom, "free woman" that she is (Gal 4:31). To be free is to be open to every cause and concern, to be so free as to be the slave of no cause or concern: that is the freedom of Christ. A tall order. Actually, a hopeless enterprise for those whose principal concern is with their own righteousness. After all is said and done, we must be willing to find ourselves with no righteousness of our own, no legal rectitude, but only with the righteousness which comes from faith in Christ, given by God in response to faith (Phil 3:9). That means, in the concrete, that the church must make discretionary judgments without trying to curry favor from people (if she did, she would be no servant of Christ!), and then cast all her cares on God, in the realization that she is his charge (Gal 1:10; 1 Pt 5:7).

Summary of the Discussion

This article grows out of several convictions. The admission of women to Holy Orders is the subject matter of a *discretionary* judgment on the part of the Episcopal Church in the United States and is not primarily a *doctrinal* matter. The fact that it is a discretionary matter implies that it is squarely *ecumenical*. It also means that it must not be put in *political* terms; if this were done, the church would be currying favor from people. Obviusly, this does not mean that there are no political aspects to the issue, nor that the eventual decision, whichever way it goes, will not have political consequences. In the concrete, there is the danger of *selective ecumenism;* the kind of ecumenism invoked to plead for or against woman's ordination is not true ecumenism at all. Hence, the Episcopal Church is called to occupy its own place among the churches, and there are reasons to count on the understanding of those churches which will continue to keep women out of the ordained ministry. Finally, the issue is ecumenical at a level that is more basic than ecumenism among the churches can ever be, viz., at the level of harmonious relationships between men and women. Let us take a closer look at these considerations.

I. *Doctrinal considerations*

Three points deserve consideration here, after it is remembered that Haye van der Meer, in his WOMEN PRIESTS IN THE CATHOLIC CHURCH? (Phila.: Temple U. P., 1973) has convincingly shown that the traditional arguments in favor of the exclusion of women from the ordained ministry must be called insufficient.

(a) First, there is the *christological* argument. The fact that Christ is a man, the argument goes, shows that, by God's own revealed will, it takes a male to preside over the church; hence, only men can convincingly represent Christ. This argument must be rejected, for it places masculinity in a privileged position in the hypostatic union of the divine nature and the human nature in the one Person of the God-Man. The tradition expressed this point as follows:

> The only thing that is *not* implied in the general terms used by Chalcedon are the individual characteristics. For that reason the saying "what is not assumed is not redeemed" may be understood only of the specific nature [i.e. the "human nature"] and not of these characteristics. In other words, Christ would not have to be a woman, an atomic physicist, or a Japanese in order to be redeemer for women, atomic physicists, and Japanese.[1]

Hence, all human persons can become the bearers of Christ's person and of his ministries, which is the same as saying that women *can* be ordained.

(b) Second, there is the *theological* argument. God, it is said, is consistently named by the name of "Father", and the usage of Jesus confirms this in such a way as to make the metaphor normative; hence only men can convincingly act in the role of mediator between people and God. Now it must be clear from the outset that this does not make God masculine, since the divine essence, as especially St. Gregory of Nyssa has taught, is incomprehensible and transcendent, surpassing all differentiations. The question, in other words, is not whether God is masculine or not, but whether he can be credibly represented only by masculine metaphors and male persons. Without in any way denying the obvious preponderance of masculine imagery in the tradition, it must still be said that the usage of Jesus must not be uncritically taken as normative in this regard. Jesus calls his Father *Abba,* which is a name expressing endearment. In other words, it is the unprecedented tone of familiarity, and not the masculine metaphor in and of itself, that expresses the unique relationship of Jesus to the Father — a relationship which Christians are called to participate in. There is no doctrinal reason why women could not, in the Lord, be the sacramental representatives of our God, who calls us to such intimacy.[2]

(c) The only doctrine that applies to the issue is the doctrine of the inclusive unity of the Body of Christ implied in the baptismal formula of Gal 3:28: "As many of you as were baptized into Christ have put on Christ. There is . . . neither male nor female; for you are all one in Christ Jesus." What does this doc-

trine mean? It does *not* mean: women *must* be ordained. So the
fact that they have not been ordained in the tradition of some
of the mainstream churches is not a departure from sound doctrine. Doctrine, in and of itself, does not put the church under
any obligation. "Of course we all 'have knowledge'." But "this
knowledge breeds conceit; it is love that builds" (1 Cor 8:1).
Love must decide the issue. This love takes the shape of discretionary ecclesiastical judgment if the issue affects the church
as a whole.[3]

II. *Discretionary matters as ecumenical matters*

Ordination of women to the priesthood is possible from the
doctrinal point of view. But this knowledge does not put the
church under any obligation, any more than the correct realization that "an idol has no real existence" put the Corinthians
under the obligation to disregard completely the conscientious
overtones of the eating of meat offered to idols (1 Cor 8:1 - 13;
10:23 - 11:1).

This is so because good Christian practice can never *in its
concreteness* be deduced from sound doctrine. Doctrine, after all,
is not a stable, one-for-all given; it is itself subject to the conditions of history, at least in the sense that there is such a thing
as development of doctrine. In the experience of the church it
has often happened that doctrine developed under the influence
of the practical, living faith-decisions of saints, inspired groups
of Christians, and others, who put vital life-issues up for mediation and theological study. Hence, good Christian practice in the
concrete has often been the source of sound doctrine rather than
the other way round.

But are there doctrines, then, which are so timeless and
essential that they remain the source of good Christian practice —
let us say, the divinity of Christ, the all-encompassing mercy of
God, etc.? If for a moment we prescind from the time-determined
formulations of such central truths, we must indeed say that
there are such doctrines. Otherwise we would lapse into complete doctrinal relativism. But then we must also realize at once
that such doctrines, precisely because of their divine character,
are inexhaustible. The church is always called to a fuller realization and to a fuller actualization of the mystery they convey.
How that fuller realization and actualization will happen *in the
concrete,* however, cannot be read off without ado from the
doctrine in its stark form. It takes concrete situations to present

the church with the kind of decision-situation that calls for a discretionary judgment — a judgment which at once changes the church's practice and gives her a deeper realization of the depths of mystery involved in the doctrine. But to take this position means that practical decisions and discretionary judgments are part and parcel of the church's realization of what is involved in doctrine.

What is the shape which such discretionary judgments tend to take when the church as a whole is involved? The answer is: they are concretized in church order. But then we must be immediately reminded that the church order only conveys its real meaning, i.e. its Christian meaning, if it is seen against the background of what gave rise to it in the first place, viz. the practice of *agape,* born of the desire to do justice to concrete needs and to show concern for the weak and the wronged. That means: the discretionary judgments that make up the church order are only intelligible if they promote communion and are perceived as such. Hence the emphasis, from the earliest times, on *koinonia* and *communio,* or, to use the Russian Orthodox term, *sobornost.* The subjective attitudes that animate this communion are mutual respect and understanding, a willingness not to be doctrinaire (*epikeia*), a sense that we are to deal with each other, not as the slaves of doctrinal or legal tyranny, but as members of one family, of one household (*oikonomia*) .[4]

This in turn means that the decision about the admission of women to the ordained priesthood in the Episcopal Church is squarely *ecumenical,* since it involves a practical, discretionary judgment which is also going to affect the Episcopal Church's relationships — at the level of church order — with the other churches. In the practical situation of incomplete unity among the churches such a discretionary judgment becomes very important, so that the question becomes: how is the decision going to affect the unity of Christians?

III. *A political approach?*

Communio, like the entire ecumenical enterprise, is far more than politics, or the art of the feasible. The goal of ecumenism is not an easy truce among the churches at the level of church order, but rather the union of all Christians in the Lord. Any attempt to force such a truce would very probably exclude a sizable part of the Christian world — political settlements tend to have victims! The ecumenical enterprise would degenerate into pure politics if the different church orders were taken for the *main* object of comparison, negotiation, mutual adaptation, and harmonization, without keeping in mind that those church orders represent discretionary faith-and-*agape* judgments about the very nature of the church. This can even be maintained with regard to elements in the order of a particular church which I would consider objectively heretical; unless I manage to see and appreciate the faith-inspiration behind such an element I am in no position to exercise the *theological,* ecumenical virtue of acceptance and an understanding (and confrontation!) in the Lord.[5]

Each church's loyalty in matters ecumenical is to the Lord, not to any particular church order, whether it be its own or that of other churches. Neither the tradition nor the practice of any church must be canonized, although they can be usefully employed in the service of testing a new issue. If the traditions of any church were canonized as such, ecumenism would become a purely political (and terribly painful) exercise in harmonization and negotiation at the level of church order, in which each church would agree to having some of its feathers singed in the interest of a type of unity that would amount to little more than forced uniformity. In addition, in such a process, many if not all churches would find themselves truckling to the orders of other churches and second-guessing the responses of other churches, and thus they would be continually tempted to curry favor from people, rather than seeking the will of the Lord in the matter of Christian unity.[6]

This is, of course, not the same as saying that there are no political aspects to the issue. The decision of the Episcopal Church, whichever way it goes, will have consequences for its relationships to other churches at the level of church order. I like to think that an affirmative decision would mean a lot to the ordained women ministers, say, in the United Methodist Church and the United Church of Christ, given the high visibility and authoritative status the ordained clergy in the Episcopal Church have traditionally enjoyed. An affirmative decision would also, I like to think, be a forceful invitation extended to such churches as the Roman Catholic Church and the various Orthodox Churches to confront the issue of the role of women in the church. But it would be as wrong for the Episcopal Church to make an affirmative decision for such reasons as it would be wrong not to make it because of some flack from "Rome" or "Constantinople". The fact that, in the ecumenical situation, all churches find themselves responsible, in the Lord, for each other does not mean that the churches are also responsible for each other's *responses*.

IV. *Selective ecumenism*

I must be frank now. In the concrete, an affirmative decision made by the Episcopal Church in the matter of the admission of women to the ordained priesthood would raise issues mainly between the Episcopal Church and the Roman Catholic, Old Catholic, and Orthodox Churches. I say this because I think that the main sources of opposition to women's ordinations in the Episcopal Church are the concerns that animate such movements as the American Church Union.

It must be stated from the outset that the American Church Union is in some ways the direct descendant of the Tractarian movement, which, more than any other movement, has helped to place the Anglican Communion in the mediating position in the ecumenical movement that it has today. In other words: its tradition entitles the A.C.U. to raise the issue of ecumenism in the context of the matter in hand. But it must also be said: the Anglican Communion *as a whole* is the heir of the Tractarian movement, and *it* can claim to be its rightful representative, for the Anglican Communion would not be what it is without the powerful doctrinal, ascetical, and ecclesiological impetus of Pusey, Keble, Newman, and so many others. Its impact on the Roman Catholic Church is notable not only in the person and influence of Newman, but also in the concerns brought forward and adopted in the course of the Second Vatican Council.

This means first of all that it would be inappropriate and untruthful for members of the A.C.U. to think of themselves and their tradition merely as the representatives of Roman Catholic and Orthodox concerns within the Episcopal Church; they are also representatives of an *Anglican* tradition that has caused significant changes in the doctrinal and ecclesial stance of the *Roman Catholic* Church.

It also means that it would be a misperception of the factual course of history if the A.C.U. were to present themselves as the only representatives of the Tractarians, and it would be inappropriate for them to act as if they were the only members of the Episcopal Church to be actually responsible for good relation-

ships with "Rome" and "Constantinople".[7] While finding myself, as a Roman Catholic, in profound sympathy with many
aspects of A.C.U. sensibility in matters doctrinal, ecclesiological
and ascetical, I cannot get myself, as a Catholic theologian, to
relate to the Anglican Communion only through the mediation
of the concerns represented by the A.C.U. and those Christians
in the Anglican Churches who see themselves as primarily inspired by the Tractarian tradition.

Hence, there is no reason now to defend the exclusion of
women from the priesthood in the Episcopal Church under in-
vocation of "Rome" and "Constantinople". It just may be the
vocation of the Anglican Communion once again to be the in-
strument in God's hand to enlighten *them* on this particular
score.

Such an appeal to "Rome" and "Constantinople" is often,
as we have said, put forward as an act of ecumenical concern, and
it often is. But not necessarily or in every respect. It may, in fact,
be unecumenical. The latter would be the case if it were implied
that ecumenism would primarily (and even exclusively) impel
the Episcopal Church to reach out to Rome, Constantinople, and
Utrecht, thus relegating the great majority of Christian churches
to a "Low" — what a metaphor! — status. This would be nothing
short of an attitude of "selective ecumenism" — which in fact
would be no ecumenism at all.

V. *Can the Episcopal Church occupy its own place and count on understanding?*

If the soul of ecumenism is *agape, communio, koinonia, sobornost,* then harmony at the level of church order becomes a
relative good. This means: the Episcopal Church is primarily
called to occupy *its own place* among the Christian churches,
with its own church order, developed in function of the concrete
signs of the times as they appear within and around the Episcopal
Church. There lies its loyalty to the Lord who is to come.

The question of women's ordination to the priesthood is
indeed an ecumenical issue, but this means that it must be approached, not from the point of view of the various orders of
other churches, but from the point of view of *communio*.

Hence, the question becomes: can the Episcopal Church
count on the Roman Catholic Church, the Orthodox Churches,
and the Old Catholic Church to be respectful and understand-

ing, willing not to be doctrinaire, ready to approach the Episcopal Church with *oikonomia?*

I do not venture to speak for Orthodoxy, nor for Old Catholics, although I have reason to suspect, in view of the long tradition of *epikeia* and *oikonomia* that characterizes Orthodoxy at its best, that there will be understanding from those quarters. I do not venture to speak even for the Roman Catholic Church, because I lack any hierarchical qualification; I can only speak as a Catholic priest and as a Catholic theologian. My expectation (and my hope) is that the Roman Catholic Church will be understanding. My reasons are twofold.

First, although recent statements on the role of women in the church's ministry have still firmly rejected the participation of women as ministers in the church's sacramental liturgy, this rejection has been based on tradition rather than on any idea that women are essentially incapable of being part of the church's ordained ministry. The ancient thesis: "Only the male can be the proper subject of ordination," is obviously now understood to express a discipline, not an essential incapacity.

Secondly—and more directly ecumencially—post-Vatcian II ecclesiology has moved steadily away from a conception of the unity of all Christian churches in terms of unity of church order, in the direction of collegiality, relative local autonomy, unity in diversity, and even in the direction of a communion of a variety of "rites". This "synodal", "pluriform" orientation of Roman Catholic ecclesiology — combined with a sustained emphasis on the Pope as visible center of Christian unity, but with the "monarchy" metaphor toned down — warrants the expectation that the ordination of women to the priesthood in the Episcopal Church will not turn out to be an insuperable obstacle to harmonious ecumenical relationships with Rome.

VI. *"You are all one in Christ Jesus" (Gal. 3:28)*

Oikoumene originally means "the inhabited earth." Without pressing etymology to the point where "ecumenism" would "really mean" the process of making the earth inhabitable, it does make sense to point out that ecumenism must press further than merely ecclesiastical concerns. The ordination of women to the priesthood is but one way in which a larger, more basic, more comprehensive concern is raised, namely, the need, in the Lord, for harmonious relationships between men and women, not only in friendships and marriages and good professional collegiality, but also in social structures. The raising of the issue of discrimination against women in the world at large as well as in the church must, from a theological point of view, be seen as an instance of historical revelation, and as such it is the work of the Holy Spirit in the world as well as in the church. Through this process of consciousness-raising it has now more than ever become possible to accept the gift of redemption from the debilitating cultural prejudice against women, which is a social sin that has held men and women captives for so long. Without the church's commitment to absorb and outsuffer and so to redeem the hurts and the scars of this affliction, a decision to ordain women to the priesthood would be the worst kind of ecclesiastical tokenism. *With* such a commitment — which would have to show itself in countless (and delicate) other ways as well — it could be a blessing which would make the earth more inhabitable for all of us.

NOTES

1 Piet Schoonenberg, THE CHRIST (N.Y.: Herder & Herder, 1971), pp. 72-73.

2 Cp. "Invalid or Merely Irregular? — Comments by a Reluctant Witness," *Journal of Ecumenical Studies* XI (1974) 381 - 399, p. 398, n. 45.

3 An example of this in history is the practice of the medieval Church to withhold the chalice from lay people. Much as we may now disagree with that decision (which grew over a long period of time), we must recognize that this was a discretionary matter. Hence, the argument of some reformers that this practice amounted to the exclusion of the laity from the "true sacrament" is a doctrinaire overstatement, a sample of conceit bred by "knowledge".

4 Cp. "Towards an Ecumenical Understanding of the Sacraments," *Journal of Ecumenical Studies* III (1966) 57 - 112, pp. 111 - 112.

5 I do not mean to exclude the possibility that the issue of women's ordination to the priesthood could be used to "solve" a different problem, again in a purely political fashion, viz. by the church's making an easy settlement with women's liberation. This issue is outside the scope of this paper, but let me point out two things. First, the church could much better and much more critically deal with feminism if women were in the ordained ministry ("What is not assumed is not saved"!). Secondly, just as racist institutions tend to hire unqualified blacks, because they are mainly interested in salving their own guilty consciences and promoting a liberal image, so sexist institutions have a tendency to employ unqualified women. In both cases the final outcome is the same: the performance of the blacks, or the women, is below par, and the institution finds a new rationale for its racist or sexist prejudices. This comparison must not be taken to imply that the racial problem and the sexism problem are the same, but that a purely political approach to either leads to analogous undesirable results.

6 The background for the position here taken is the idea that ecumenism is not retrospective, but prospective and eschatological. Cp. *op. cit.,* n. 4, pp. 69 - 73.

7 Alleged utterances by some prominent Roman Catholic and Orthodox churchmen ("It would sever all ties." — "They won't do it, for they put too high a value on good relationships with us." — Etc.), while doubtlessly born out of serious conviction, sound a little bit like veiled threats — to which especially those in the Episcopal Church who feel close ties with Rome and with Orthodoxy may easily give in. 1 Cor 4:3 - 4 is the watchword in such cases.

9 The Existing Canonical Authority for Women's Ordination

Henry H. Rightor

There are no canonical or constitutional barriers to the ordination of women to the diaconate, priesthood or episcopate in the Protestant Episcopal Church in the U.S.A.

The canonical situation here calls to mind the judgment of Samuel Johnson regarding the strawberry: "Doubtless God could have made a better berry than the strawberry; but doubtless God never did." In the same vein one can say that doubtless General Convention, the governing body of the Episcopal Church in the United States, could have enacted barriers to the ordination of women; but doubtless General Convention never did. Down through the years Convention has exercised its authority to restrict ordination to each of the three orders of ministry to persons with various qualifications, such as age; but one searches in vain for a constitutional or canonical restriction of ordination to males in any of the three orders.

The Constitution, Canons and Ordinal generally refer to persons in all Holy Orders by words of male gender. Where the context of the words is not violated, however, this church and its convention, like the civil courts, have always given a generic interpretation to such words as "man," "brother" and the referent pronouns "he," "him" and "his." This has been true with regard to both the canons and the liturgy. If an example were needed, there is the familiar creedal phrase, "for us men and for our salvation." To say that females are not included in the word "men" would be considered outrageous.

In one instance the House of Clerical and Lay Deputies of General Convention, acting apart from the House of Bishops, departed from the general rule of generic interpretation which includes females in words of male gender. At the 1949 Convention the Deputies, using their exclusive authority to judge the qualifications of the members of that House, ruled that women who had been elected Lay Deputies were not "laymen." This ruling meant that women did not meet the constitutional requirement that only "laymen" could serve as Lay Deputies.[1]

The arbitrary nature of the House of Deputies' restriction of "laymen" to male deputies is apparent from the history of that same House. At the preceding Convention in 1946 the identical issue was raised when the qualifications of a woman elected a Deputy to that Convention were questioned for the same reason. Serving as a Lay Deputy from New York at the 1946 Convention was an eminent jurist, the Hon. Augustus N. Hand. He urged the House of Deputies to follow the normal practice of interpreting "laymen" as a generic word which includes females, and Mrs. Randolph H. Dyer of Missouri was seated as a Lay Deputy.[2]

The question of seating women as Lay Deputies remained subject to the arbitrary interpretation of the House of Deputies until 1970. In that year a constitutional amendment removed the question from the jurisdiction of the House of Deputies by changing the word "layman" to "lay person" in the article defining the qualifications of Lay Deputies.

The obvious method of restricting generic words so as to exclude females is to use the word "male" in a particular canon or constitutional provision. For example, the office of lay reader was restricted by canon to "males" until 1969. However, the General Conventions of both 1970 and 1973 failed to take the obvious steps to end the debate regarding the ordination of women; either of those Conventions could have restricted by canon the diaconate, or the priesthood, or the episcopate, or any two or three of the orders to "males," had this been the intent of either Convention. It can not seriously be argued that the House of Deputies' failure, in those years, to adopt resolutions favoring the ordination of women to the priesthood had the effect of restricting that order to males. The vote each time was a Vote by Orders and by Dioceses.

Note on the Vote by Orders and by Dioceses

Article I, Section 4 of the Constitution provides that on "any question" a majority vote of the Deputies present shall suffice unless a higher number is called for by the Constitution or the Canons, or "unless the Clerical or the Lay representation from any Diocese require that the vote be taken by orders. In all cases of a vote by orders, the two orders shall vote separately, each Diocese and Missionary Diocese having one vote in the Clerical order and one vote in the Lay order." A majority of the Dioceses voting affirmatively on the question in both orders is necessary for its passage.

Every Diocese is normally represented by its full complement of four Clerical and four Lay Deputies. The vote of a diocesan deputation in one or both orders is often divided, with two votes for and two against the proposed question. The attainment of a majority vote in both orders, necessary for passage of a question, would not be too difficult if the diocesan deputations with divided votes were treated as having abstained from voting; these deputations would not then be included in the number of which a majority is required for passage.

Attainment of a majority vote on a question is made substantially more difficult, however, by Rule 41 of the Rules of Procedure in the House of Deputies. This Rule states that the votes of diocesan deputations in each order are recorded as "Aye," "No," or "Divided." So long as the divided deputations are included in the number of which a majority is required for passage of a question, a "Divided" vote has the same effect as a "No" vote. Thus a 2 - 2 vote in any deputation is no different from a 3 - 1 or 4 - 0 "No" vote, with regard to the outcome of a proposed resolution on a vote by orders and by dioceses.

Chancellor Arthur W. Machen, Jr., of the Diocese of Maryland, has written an essay entitled "General Convention Voting Procedures or — The Strange Game of Episcopal Roulette." He simplifies his analysis by assuming a House of Deputies composed of 1,000 members, with 500 clerical and 500 lay deputies from 125 dioceses, rather than the 113 dioceses represented at the 1973 Convention. Regarding the vote by orders he concluded: "All it takes is two votes in either order from 63 dioceses, or 126 deputies out of a total of 500 in that order, to cause that order to be totally divided. Thus, the question could fail by a negative vote as meager as 25.2% of one order or 12.6% of the entire House.

"On a constitutional question requiring a two-thirds vote, the power of the minority is even more startling. In our hypothetical House of 125 dioceses, a minimum of 84 must vote affirmatively in *both* orders for the proposal to pass, and it takes only 42 diocesan votes in *either* order to defeat it. It follows that only two deputies from any of 42 dioceses, or a total of 84 out of 500 in either order can block anything. These numbers represent less than 17% of either order and less than 9% of the entire House."

The vote by orders and by dioceses in the House of Deputies makes it possible for a relatively small minority in either the clerical or the lay order to vote down any resolution. The tallies in both the 1970 and the 1973 Conventions on the resolution favoring the ordination of women demonstrate an interesting fact: had a contrary resolution been presented, that is, had the resolution favored the restriction of the priesthood to males, it too would have been defeated at both Conventions — and by a much larger vote. The point is that the simple failure of the Deputies to pass any such resolution, whether the resolution favors ordaining women or whether it favors restricting ordination to males, is precatory at best. (Bishops and Dioceses have always remained free to reject the "askings" of Convention. For instance, the diocesan authorities of New Mexico and Southwest Texas refused in 1969 to pay to the national church its quota, the "asking" made of it by Convention, because they did not like one grant made from the General Convention Special Program.) Surely the failure of the Deputies to adopt a resolution favoring the ordination of women to the priesthood has none of the obligatory effect of a canon, enacted by the entire Convention, restricting that order to males; and, without such restriction by Convention, the normal interpretation of generic words assumes the inclusion of females in the relevant constitutional, canonical and liturgical provisions for ordination.

The general rule of including females in generic words was in no way affected, where their ordination is concerned, by the rule of construction included in Canons III. 2 and 3, adopted in 1973. These canons have to do with Candidates for Holy Orders, and Section 1 of both canons recites that "words of male gender shall also imply female gender."

Note on the Effect of the Generic Interpretation of Words
of Male Gender Having Been Expressed in Canons III. 2 and 3

The General Convention of 1973 adopted Canons III. 2 and 3, written by an *ad hoc* committee of which the author of this essay was a member. Section 1 of each Canon says: "This Canon shall be interpreted in its plain and literal sense, except that words of male gender shall also imply the female gender." Canon 2 is entitled "Of

Candidates for Holy Orders"; Canon 3, "Of the Normal Standard of Learning and Examination of Candidates for Holy Orders."

In documents such as wills, the express grant of a certain object or sum of money to a particular devisee can be held to bar the devisee's claim that the devisor intended the devisee to receive additional objects or sums. The rejection of the claim would accord with the maxim, "expressio unis est exclusio alterius"; the mention of one thing implies the exclusion of another. However, the mention of generic construction of words of male gender in two particular canons could not, by this or any other principle of interpretation, be considered to exclude the generic construction of the same words throughout the entire body of canons, enacted serially over a period of many years.[3]

The recitation of the rule of construction in Canons III. 2 and 3 did not create the rule, nor did it limit application of the rule to the instances where it was expressed. The recitation of the rule of generic construction is, rather, similar to the practice of printing "he" in italics in the Baptismal Service and, more recently, in the Confirmation Service of the Book of Common Prayer. The rules of construction in the two canons that came before the 1973 Convention for adoption were helpful reminders that no debate regarding women's ordination was necessary to their passage. The different print of "he" in the Baptismal and Confirmation Services did not create its generic nature in these services; such print is, rather, a helpful reminder to clergy to substitute "she" when the person involved is female. (A thorough dicussion of the use of different type in these instances appears in *Board of Presenters v. Wendt*, Diocese of Washington, 1975, p. 15.)

Seriously to affirm that a rule of construction is necessary for each canon regarding the ordained ministry to permit the generic interpretation of words of male gender — or to maintain that "women" must be specifically mentioned in such canons before they apply to females — would produce absurd results. It would mean, for example, that those women whose ordination to the diaconate is now unquestioned could not be disciplined in any way under the existing canons; for all of the canons regarding ecclesiastical discipline use words of male gender exclusively, and these words require a generic interpretation if they are to apply to women.

Note on Canon III. 26, "Of Women and the Diaconate"

A unique and unrelated instance of the specific mention of "women" in a canon regarding their ordination to a particular order

of ministry is found in Canon III. 26, "Of Women and the Diaconate." This canon was adopted in 1970 to replace old Canon 50, "On
Deaconesses," pursuant to the recommendation in the Report to the
1970 Convention by the Joint Commission on Women Church Workers.[4] . . . Resolution I recommended by the Commission proposed that
existing deaconesses "be declared to be within the Diaconate." This
resolution was adopted by Convention separately from the succeeding
resolutions recommended by the Commission.[5] . . . The succeeding
resolutions were adopted as new Canon III. 26, replacing old Canon
50.[6] The intent of the new canon, read in conjunction with the resolution declaring deaconesses to be within the diaconate, was clear: it
was to permit women who wished to serve permanently in the more
limited order of ministry to continue to do so in the diaconate rather
than as "deaconesses." It is for this reason that Section 5 of Canon
III. 26 made it possible for such women to be exempted from the
provisions relating to the priesthood in requirements for postulants
and candidates for Holy Orders.

There are those who would agree with all the foregoing
statements in this article, but who are disturbed by the fact that
those who wrote and adopted most of the constitutional and
canonical provisions regarding ordination did not have women
in mind. Those who are hesitant, for this reason, to see women
ordained to the priesthood or episcopate are due a respectful
answer. For in the interpretation of some documents, a will
being a fair example, the intent of the author at the time of
writing is often conclusive.

A will is a "dead" document, however, compared to a
constitution and the laws or canons it controls. In societies informed by the Anglo-American common law, constitutions

> must be read as embodying general principles meant to
> govern society and institutions of government *as they
> evolve through time*. It is therefore this Court's function
> to apply the Constitution as *a living document* to the
> legal cases and controversies of contemporary society.[7]

This quotation is from the opinion of a three-judge Federal
Court in Alabama, where a civil suit successfully depended on
the equal protection clause of the 14th Amendment to attack
an Alabama statute stating that only "male residents of the
County" were qualified for jury service. The defense contended,
unsuccessfully, that "the 14th Amendment was not historically
intended to require the states to make women eligible for jury
service."

It is suggested here that the several dioceses of this church, by virtue of their existing canonical authority, need not wait for further action by General Convention to ordain women to the priesthood. They are called on by our tradition to look beyond the historical intent of the Constitution and Canons, and to treat them as "living documents," to be applied "to the controversies of contemporary society."

Note on the Use of Analogues from Civil Law to Interpret the Constitution and Canons of the Church.

Strictly speaking, there is no Canon "Law" in the Protestant Episcopal Church in the U.S.A. comparable to that in the Church of England and other Established Churches, whether Anglican or not. The Constitution and Canons of the Episcopal Church in this country more nearly resemble the by-laws of a voluntary association, which depend for their context on the civil law which surrounds them. It is this context of civil law which justifies the use of civil law analogues to interpret the Church's Constitution and Canons.

The use of the civil law context is expressly validated in Canon IV. 3, Sec. 21, regarding Courts and their Procedures, as follows:

Sec. 21. In the conduct of investigations preliminary to presentments, as well as in all trials, the laws of the civil jurisdiction in which such investigation or trial is had, so far as they relate to evidence, shall be adopted and taken as the rules by which said Board of Inquiry, Commission, or Court, shall be governed, and trials shall be conducted according to the principles of the common law as the same is generally administered in the United States, except in those Dioceses where Ecclesiastical Courts are provided for by Constitution or Statute, in which case the same shall govern.

In White and Dykman's ANNOTATED CONSTITUTION AND CANONS (Greenwich, Conn.: Seabury Press, 1954, Vol. II, p. 323) there is the following terse commentary on the exception made in the above canon for provision for ecclesiastical courts by a civil constitution or statute: "An exception is made for dioceses where ecclesiastical courts are provided for by constitution or statute, *of which there are none"* [Emphasis added].

Conclusion

It is submitted that no action by General Convention is required to give a Diocesan the authority to ordain a female deacon to the priesthood under Canon III. 11, given the recommendation of the Standing Committee of the Diocese and the required certificate from the Minister and Vestry of the Parish where she resides. The same authority, presently existing, also permits Diocesans to regularize the ordination of the female deacons ordained to the priesthood in Philadelphia on July 29, 1974, and in Washington, D.C., on September 7, 1975.[8]

At the 1973 General Convention the House of Bishops seems to have been well aware that authority to ordain women deacons to the priesthood did, in fact, exist. For, to prevent any such ordinations, a majority of the Bishops resorted to an alarming expedient on the last afternoon of the Convention; by a vote of 53 to 40 they invoked "the principle of collegiality," in an apparent effort to intimidate individual bishops who might otherwise exercise their authority to ordain women to the priesthood. The entire resolution is set out herewith:

> WHEREAS, The House of Deputies has, in this 64th General Convention, rejected the principle of the ordination of women to the priesthood; and
>
> WHEREAS, The Presiding Bishop-elect has called for the appointment of a competent committee to study in depth the matter of the ordination of women; and
>
> WHEREAS, It has been said that individual Bishops have expressed their intention to ordain women to the priesthood in spite of the action of the House of Deputies; therefore, be it
>
> RESOLVED, That the House of Bishops put these rumors to rest by a public affirmation of its adherence to the principles of collegiality and mutual loyalty, as well as respect for due constitutional and canonical process.[9]

"Collegiality" does not appear in the church's Constitution, Canons or Ordinal, nor has it been found in any index of prior resolutions of General Convention or the House of Bishops. The adjective "collegial" had been used previously only once, when new Rule XXV was adopted as a rule of order by the House of Bishops in 1970.[10] "Collegial" is there used in a precise and understandable way: to describe the kind of membership in the House of Bishops that may be given a Bishop of a church in the Anglican communion, resident in a jurisdiction of this church. The "collegial" member, under Rule XXV, is admitted on a two-thirds vote of the House and given a seat and voice, but no vote.

Clearly the House of Bishops has never been given the power to invest the "principle of collegiality" with any such arcane meaning as has been given it by the Bishops of this church since 1973. Those Bishops who participated in the Philadelphia ordinations of 1974, and the Washington ordinations of 1975, refused to be bound by the new "principle of collegiality." However, this principle has been allowed by other bishops to override their canonical authority to ordain women to the priesthood and to regularize the irregular ordinations that have already taken place. The surrender of episcopal authority and responsibility to the "principle of collegiality" is admittedly true of several Bishops who are both conscious of their canonical authority and desirous of ordaining qualified women to the priesthood.

Some Bishops have indicated that they feel restrained by "collegiality" only through the forthcoming 1976 Convention, after which they will begin ordaining women even if Convention fails to act. Because they are aware of their existing authority to ordain women to the priesthood, the action they seek must be action by the House of Bishops, rather than action by General Convention as a whole. It was not Convention but the House of Bishops which imposed the restraints of "collegiality" on its members at the close of the 1973 Convention; and it is obvious that only that House can remove them if, indeed, they do exist.

The "principle of collegiality," as it has been employed, remains an offense to the Protestant Episcopal Church in the U.S.A. whether its duration is indefinite, or whether it is only to be honored between the meetings of the House of Bishops which take place at General Convention. The offense does not lie in the respect which members of the House of Bishops properly show each other; it lies in the fact that the "principle of collegiality," adopted by one House of General Convention, should arbitrarily be used to override the Constitution and Canons of this Church for *any* length of time. The maxim, "justice delayed is justice denied," applies to ecclesiastical as well as to civil institutions.

There remains one area, not strictly canonical, in which a resolution by Convention favoring the ordination of women to the priesthood would be not necessary, but helpful. The Anglican Consultative Council has advised that a Bishop should have the approval of his "Province" (in this Church, General Convention) before such ordinations take place in any diocese of the Anglican Communion. The advice and requests of that Council, like those of the Lambeth Conference, are due great respect; this, although their requests and advice have no binding control over the actions of any church in the Anglican Communion.

There comes a time, however, when the Christian mission of a church takes precedence over things a particular church might like to do. Today seems to be such a time in the life of this church, when its mission to men as well as women is hampered by the arbitrary treatment of women as less than full members of the Body of Christ. This treatment continues so long as women are denied access to the priesthood. The mission of this church demands that they receive *now*, not at some uncertain time in the future, the regular ordination now permitted them by the church's Constitution and Canons.

NOTES

1 JOURNAL OF GENERAL CONVENTION, 1949; p. 102.
2 JOURNAL OF GENERAL CONVENTION, 1946; p. 102.
3 Cf. 73 *American Jurisprudence 2d,* "Statutes," Sec. 212, together with cases cited.
4 JOURNAL OF GENERAL CONVENTION, 1970; pp. 769 - 70.
5 *Op. cit.,* p. 270.
6 *Op. cit.,* p. 249.
7 *White v. Crook,* 251 F. Supp. 401 (1956). (Emphasis added.)
8 Cf. *Standing Committee v. Beebe,* Diocese of Ohio, 1975.
9 JOURNAL OF GENERAL CONVENTION, 1973; p. 124.
10 JOURNAL OF GENERAL CONVENTION, 1970; p. 77.

CONTRIBUTORS

Reginald H. Fuller is Professor of New Testament at Virginia Theological Seminary. The most recent of his many books is PREACHING THE NEW LECTIONARY. He has lectured widely on the ordination of women.

Frederick H. Borsch is Dean of the Church Divinity School of the Pacific, and formerly was Professor of New Testament at General Theological Seminary.

Lloyd G. Patterson is W. R. Huntingdon Professor of Historical Theology at the Episcopal Divinity School in Cambridge. His special interest is in the patristic period, and he is the author of GOD AND HISTORY IN EARLY CHRISTIAN THOUGHT.

Arthur A. Vogel, Bishop of West Missouri, was formerly Professor of Systematic Theology and Apologetics at Nashotah House. As a member of the Theology Committee of the House of Bishops, he wrote the report on the ordination of the Philadelphia Eleven. An abbreviated and amended version of this paper was distributed to the House of Bishops of the Episcopal Church in June, 1973, a year before the Philadelphia ordinations.

Urban T. Holmes is Dean of the School of Theology at the University of the South, and has written and lectured extensively on the ordination of women, and is joint editor with Ruth Tiffany Barnhouse, of the Presiding Bishop's study on priesthood and sexuality.

James E. Griffiss is Professor of Philosophical and Systematic Theology and Sub-Dean at Nashotah House. He was a consultant to the Theology Committee of the House of Bishops at their June, 1975 meeting.

Ruth Tiffany Barnhouse is a Clinical Assistant in Psychiatry at Harvard University, Visiting Lecturer in Pastoral Theology at Weston College School of Theology, and one of the editors of CHRISTIAN APPROACHES TO SEXUALITY, part of the Presiding Bishop's study on Priesthood and sexuality.

Frans Jozeph van Beeck, S.J., is Professor of Theology at Boston College. His view on validity was cited in Bishop Vogel's statement on the Philadelphia ordinations.

Henry H. Rightor is Arthur Lee Kinsolving Professor of Pastoral Care at Virginia Theological Seminary. Following Harvard Law School and prior to his ordination he was a practicing lawyer in Arkansas.